D1497795

LINCOLN STEFFENS

MODERN LITERATURE MONOGRAPHS
GENERAL EDITOR: Lina Mainiero

In the same series:

(continued on page 168)

LINCOLN STEFFENS

Robert Stinson

FREDERICK UNGAR PUBLISHING CO.
NEW YORK

Library of Congress Cataloging in Publication Data

Stinson, Robert, 1941–

    Lincoln Steffens.
    (Modern literature monographs)
    Bibliography: p.
    Includes index.
    1. Steffens, Joseph Lincoln, 1866–1936. 2. Journalists
—United States—Biography.
PN4874.S68S7   070.4′092′4 [B]   79–4831
ISBN 0–8044–2829–8

Contents

Chronology

1

●●●

Student and Teacher

Lincoln Steffens adopted a variety of personae during a lifetime of popular writing, but his most consistent pose was that of student. To be sure, he thought himself a teacher as well, and all his life after publishing a story or giving a lecture he wondered whether, in his own casual phrase, his readers or audience had "got it." But more than anything else he was, to himself, a student. *The Autobiography of Lincoln Steffens* (1931), surely his best if not his best-known work, is the most conspicuous carrier of his student motif, though the image is central to virtually all his work.

As recounted in his *Autobiography*, the lifelong apprenticeship to living begins and ends in optimism, but the experience itself and Steffens's thinking about it were often tinged with resentment. His was a "life of unlearning" he told many people, including his publisher when he tried to argue that phrase into the book's title, and what unlearning meant was that his education had fallen into two parts: first, the boyhood acceptance of myths about society, human behavior and especially the motives for behavior; and then the slow, painful discovery through experience with life that the storybooks were lies and that the world was peopled with "bad" men who seemed good and "good" men who were bad. Well before he thought of writing his autobiography, in fact, he liked to include in speeches about public affairs the statement that he spent the first twenty-four years of his life being "educated" and the next twenty-four getting "the cultured lies out of my head." [1]

Every writer—indeed, every person—can match with his own life a youthful disillusionment roughly corresponding to Steffens's. But what made his experience unique was, as he imagined it, that the unlearning took nearly a lifetime to complete. Hence the tone of resentment in the *Autobiography* and also in some of the letters as his education progressed. Not until close to the end would he throw off the last of his naiveté, too late to do anything but declare that his life had nevertheless been worth the living and to write a long book—the two-volume, 873-page *Autobiography*—for his son and all youth to read as a manual for avoiding error themselves. He was most self-consciously a student, then, an innocent made ironically the more defenseless by the lying formal education he resented all his life.

Steffens's *Autobiography* is a classic of its genre and will be taken up again for the extensive analysis it deserves. Its self-characterization of Steffens as an innocent, however, offers a significant first hold on why he wrote the way he did—why, to anticipate just a bit, so many of his characters seemed to resemble himself, naive discoverers of hidden realities. The concept of his own innocence was so strong in Steffens's mind that it became the mold into which he cast the experience of others.

In a larger sense of the word, though, and a sense he understood just as well, Steffens was a student of his times. His profession was journalism, and his insights into urban life, politics, and human character from the "gray nineties" to the Great Depression of the 1930s were revelations to middle-class readers who encountered him, learning and teaching, in the pages of magazines and newspapers everywhere.

Steffens made his name with *The Shame of the Cities*

(1904), but he "discovered" the American city a decade earlier when he went to work as a cub reporter for a New York newspaper. He had grown up in semi-rural California and liked to remember himself as a "boy on horseback." That he later helped reveal New York to New Yorkers and then St. Louis, Minneapolis and other cities to themselves and the rest of the country only means that he had first to confront the cities himself.

Despite much latter-day textbook talk about "the rise of the city" following the Civil War, cities were a driving factor in American life from the nation's start. In 1790, for example, the first census turned up 201,655 urban residents in a total population of almost four million. But cities along the Atlantic Coast and scattered throughout the inland river system exercised a guiding influence on the expanding nineteenth-century economy. And, if 201,655 urban residents constituted only about five percent of the total population in 1790, the cities were growing, their populations expanding at a faster rate than the majority rural population. By 1860 urban Americans amounted to nearly twenty percent of the total, and by 1920 they would be the new majority. Among the Northeastern states, including New York where Steffens began his career, city people reached their numerical majority as early as 1880.

The rise of the city in the late decades of the nineteenth century was less a new physical fact than a new consciousness of an old pattern. Americans from Thomas Jefferson onward had often uttered misgivings about cities, though the nineteenth century also saw the emergence of an extravagant city booster literature as well— the inflated rhetoric of commercial promotion. In 1869, however, E. L. Godkin, who would later become Steffens's first employer at the *New York Evening Post*, set a new tone by publishing an editorial, "Our Great Cities," in his prestigious journal, *The Nation*. "The influence of cities is now almost all-pervading," he announced.

They draw to them the most energetic and enterprising of the population, the greatest talent as well as the greatest wealth, the soberest and steadiest and most intelligent, as well as the most ignorant and vicious. City ideas and city standards of morality spread through the country as surely, though perhaps not as rapidly, as city fashions in dress. The closeness with which farmers' daughters now copy the cut of city women's clothes is but one symptom of the process of moral and intellectual assimilation which is going on, and which is rapidly transforming vast tracts of our territory into mere suburbs of great towns.[2]

Godkin, no lover of the evils and corruption everywhere obvious in urban America, recognized that cities were here to stay and that, like it or not, they, not some bucolic ruralism represented the nation's future. Thereafter, journalists and novelists began to pay more attention to cities. By the 1890s, Lincoln Steffens joined the growing numbers of writers like Jacob Riis, Jane Addams, William Dean Howells, Stephen Crane and Theodore Dreiser who were discovering urban America for themselves and interpreting it to their countrymen.

Immigrants, pouring into America at the rate of four million in the 1890s and eight million the next decade, were the single most important factor in building these big urban populations. Of the 11,826,000 *new* city dwellers in the twentieth century's first decade, for example, 41% were immigrants while 30% were migrants from rural places and only about 22% represented natural increase—urban people bearing urban babies. The remaining 7% were added as a result of the legal incorporation by cities of territories adjacent to them. Immigrants in such great numbers changed the sight and sound of cities. Steffens studied them in his early newspaper days, liked them, and for a time even imagined himself one of them. When he came to write *The Shame of the Cities* he would be unable to accept the common argument that political corruption was something the immigrants brought with them as though in their baggage.

Steffens was also a student of politics. He began with city politics, of course, but his lifetime of writing and political activism brought him quickly to the national level and finally to the international arena. His career embraced four decades of sustained political upheaval the like of which no one had ever seen in America. His writings are veritable catalogues of the great events from the desperate Panic of 1893 and the Spanish-American War through the Progressive revolt which began the new century, the Mexican Revolution of 1915, the First World War and the Paris Peace Conference which ended it, the Bolshevik Revolution, the rise of Fascism, and the Great Depression. Steffens knew two Presidents, Theodore Roosevelt and Woodrow Wilson (though he sometimes exaggerated the intimacy of those relationships), and he interviewed Lenin, Mussolini, and a host of lesser assorted bosses and dictators. Steffens lived with sharp consciousness through America's emergence as a world power, with all the good and evil at home and abroad that this "coming out" implied. And he saw the United States make its first halting and inadequate attempts to deal with the problems of industrial society, now controlling, now catering to a rampant capitalism.

As he studied, his own contributions to popular political thinking changed. Beginning with the assumption that local circumstances controlled local politics, he grew to see that political behavior at any level bowed to worldwide economic forces and political laws.

"A learning mind makes a good teacher," Steffens said once, and it was in that spirit—the student become mentor—that he made his contributions to popular thinking.[3] He "taught" a middle-class constituency which a revolution in publishing had made newly accessible. Beginning about the 1880's the periodical publishing industry was transformed by developments in technology and society. A new process made paper-making cheaper, while high speed presses cut printing costs, allowing publishers to take advantage of production in volume. In addition, the half-tone process enabled newspapers and magazines to publish eye-catching photographs.

Meanwhile, the late nineteenth century witnessed a new popular interest in self-improvement, and that was a powerful, if diffuse, stimulus to the publishers to supply a kind of education to masses of people who had missed more formal opportunities. Partly in response to this demand, the United States Congress gradually lowered postal rates for newspapers and magazines. Finally, and of special interest to magazines, was the rise of national consumer marketing in the late nineteenth century. Manufacturers of chocolate, soap, shoes, sewing machines and other diverse products who wanted to sell nation-wide came to the nationally circulating magazines and soon fattened their pages with lucrative advertising. What all these developments meant was that publishers could drastically cut their periodicals' single-copy price and extend circulation deeply into the middle class.

Steffens began with newspapers, but his papers, the *New York Evening Post* and the *Commercial Advertiser* never reached for the mass circulations garnered by Joseph Pulitzer's sensational *New York World* or William Randolph Hearst's *Journal*. Not until he went to *McClure's Magazine* in 1902 did Steffens's work achieve the depth and scope which made his name a household word. Whereas the thirty-five-cent *Harper's*, *Scribner's*, and *Century* had stabilized at about 150,000 circulation, *McClure's* was one of the new breed which leaped to 360,000 and was still climbing by the time Steffens joined its staff.

Steffens wrote for many magazines after that, but as his own radical thinking about cities, politics and revolution became less and less middle class, Steffens valued his access to the middle-class magazines more and more. The more he learned the more he wanted to teach, so he often worried about losing the privilege of writing in the periodicals the middle class—his students—commonly read. Once in 1918, for example, when his increasingly radical ideas about the First World War and his sympathies with the Bolshevik Revolution made finding publishers difficult, Steffens received an offer from Max Eastman, Marxist editor of *The Liberator*, to finance his trip to the Paris Peace Conference. "No, not yet," he wrote. "I may have to publish in the radical publications, but I'll not do it till I'm excluded from the middle-class magazines." [4]

Steffens's own roots were unmistakably middle class. He was born in 1866 to a family which was about to establish for itself a firm place in the middle stratum of society in Sacramento, California and was upwardly mobile throughout his childhood. His father, Joseph, Sr.* began as a bookkeeper and ended as a banker, moving his family through a succession of larger and finer houses as his fortunes improved. He mixed in politics, too, and in 1884 ran a nearly victorious campaign as the Republican candidate for governor.

Steffens's early years breathe an air of almost unclouded security. There was enough money to provide him with private schooling from preparatory school and college through three years in European universities. Indeed, financial security was something he worried about very little at any point in his life. Following his European tour, in 1892, Steffens's father cut him loose in New York City where his ship had landed him. Letters from that time show him uneasy for several months about his ability to support himself. Then, unexpectedly, in 1894 he received word that a German university friend, Johann Friedrich Krudewolf, had died leaving him accounts and

---

* Lincoln Steffens's full name was Joseph Lincoln Steffens, Jr., but he began to use his familiar pen name about 1900.

properties worth about $12,000. With that and his ability to make profitable Wall Street investments, he was never to worry about money again. (Steffens would repay Krudewolf, after a fashion, when much later he made his friend's sad and mysterious story the most brilliant set piece in his *Autobiography*.)

He also had the security of love, too much love he would recall, realizing that he was always loved by others more than he himself loved. His mother, Louisa loved him as her first born. Steffens remembered that she sometimes punished him herself for his boyish misdeeds in order to save him from what she thought would be harsher treatment at his father's hands. His sisters, Louise, Lottie, and Laura, loved him, too, often with an openness that embarrassed him. Later he would see that he had been curiously wounded by this love and also by the freely given attentions from Josephine, his first wife, Johann Krudewolf, and others. In the *Autobiography* he generalized the point:

One of the wrongs suffered by boys is that of being loved before loving. They receive so early and so freely the affection and devotion of their mothers, sisters, and teachers that they do not learn to love; and so, when they grow up and become lovers and husbands, they avenge themselves upon their wives and sweethearts. Never having had to love, they cannot; they don't know how.[5]

The single ambiguity in this boyhood security involved relations with his father. He loved him and was consciously grateful for the support Joseph Steffens gave and for the hopes with which he encouraged him. Yet the boy was always conscious that what the father could give he could also take away. Or, more fundamentally, as he expressed it in a story written in 1927 and included as Chapter III of the *Autobiography*, Steffens was aware that the things he wanted were his father's to give or not in the first place, and this sense of dependence made "A

Miserable Merry Christmas" one of his sharpest, most poignant memories as well as one of his best stories.

The story, well-known and widely anthologized, is simple. When Steffens was still in grade school his family moved to a new house, and behind the house was a stable. The boy wanted a pony of his own, and, as Christmas approached, he told his father that if he could not have a pony for Christmas he wanted nothing at all. On Christmas morning he bolted from bed to find his stocking empty but also no pony in the stable. Betrayed, he remained in the yard weeping inconsolably through a long morning while his father paced impatiently in the house. Then, hours later, a stranger rode into the yard on a horse much too small for him. " 'Say kid,' he said, 'do you know a kid named Lennie Steffens?' " The pony, of course, was his. Joseph Steffens had ordered delivery at dawn, but the man had got into a fight and missed the time by hours. Steffens's sudden joy cut a swath through his misery, but the cut was ragged, imperfect. His final paragraph expressed it best:

But that Christmas, which my father had planned so carefully, was it the best or the worst I ever knew? He often asked me that; I never could answer as a boy. I think now that it was both. It covered the whole distance from broken-hearted misery to bursting happiness—too fast. A grown-up could hardly have stood it.[6]

The tale is nicely told and shows Steffens at his most mature in rendering life experience. He was here, again, an innocent, made so in this instance by the love and security his short life had known. This was his first disillusion, and it was not much softened by the fact that the boy unwittingly set *himself* up for the blow (" 'All I want is a pony,' I said. 'If I can't have a pony, give me nothing, nothing.' "). Security, he learned, was fragile; love was abundant but was either unwilling or unavailing against the unpredictable nature of life.

One wonders why his father did not explain that the pony was only late, but perhaps, as Justin Kaplan, Steffens's biographer, says, he was stung by how quickly the boy lost faith in his providing.[7] In any case, Steffens would carry that memory irrevocably connected with an ambivalence toward his father to the end of his life. Joseph Steffens always made him feel he had to justify himself. Were his European studies worth the expense? Was a career in writing substantial enough? Letters they exchanged when Steffens was away from home were genuinely affectionate, but later when he began to question the business foundation of American life, he would also think of his father as the model for the "good," dangerous respectability and sheer authority which, he thought, was the rot of a business society.

However ambiguous was the gift of the pony, once he had it Steffens was always ready to acknowledge that his father used it to educate him. The boy rode out every day in ever-widening circles to meet a variety of humankind, including more people who would love him better than he loved in return. Formal education did not suit him. He was a student in a succession of schools but his rebelliousness made his father despair that he would ever get to the state university at Berkeley. He even made him spend a year in a military preparatory school, but Steffens used his ingenuity less for study than to break the rules. When he came up for the Berkeley entrance examination, he failed. Then, after another year with a private tutor, he knew enough Latin and Greek to gain admission to the university and spent the next four years on fraternity life, courtship, prank-playing, and desultory study. He graduated in 1889 at the bottom of his class.

His autobiographical pose required that he remember most of what the schools had taught him as lies to be unlearned. Yet he did learn some things that lasted. Thrown in the school jail for drinking, and with nothing to do with the time, he called for books and read, among

others, Herbert Spencer and Charles Darwin, the twin
foundation stones of late-nineteenth century naturalism.
Perhaps Steffens's life-long infatuation with large scale
natural laws governing social behavior and moving it
along an evolutionary track dates from this time. His year
with Evelyn Nixon, who tutored him into Berkeley and
whom Steffens would remember with an affection denied
any other teacher, taught him that all questions were
open, that no one had said anything definitive on any
subject. At Berkeley he picked up the economic deter-
minism that was just then beginning to challenge older
ideas about political motivation, and this, too, would develop in his thinking through the years.

In the summer of 1889 Steffens sailed for Europe on
what would be a three-year tour of German and French
universities. He liked the life of German *Studenten*, at
once more serious and more relaxed than what he knew
at Berkeley, and, as Justin Kaplan has pointed out,
Steffens went from a career of escaping school to becoming very nearly a professional student. Following a well-
established tradition of American sons abroad, he studied
successively at Berlin, Heidelberg, Leipzig and Paris. He
studied philosophy, with special attention to ethics, and
also psychology under the direction of Leipzig's Wilhelm
Wundt, the empiricist who insisted that psychological
phenomena—sensation, perception, reaction—were either
physically measurable or did not exist. His theories had
already spread to America and would lead toward the
twentieth-century psychology of behaviorism. It was in
Wundt's laboratory that Steffens met Josephine Bontecou,
whom he fell in love with and secretly married the following year.

Because the *Autobiography* tends to simplify and ab-
stract this period as a series of brief steps in Steffens's unlearning, the best source for these years are the letters he
addressed to his father and mother, sisters and friends
at home. And the letters tell us something of special in-

terest about his early development as a writer because
they were, in a sense, early "works." He often wrote them
with an idea of their permanence, telling his middle sister, Lottie, for example, "I want to make all my letters
when brought together a complete whole. . . ." [8] Sometimes they were extended essays on the life and character of a city or a reflection on art or ethics which he
would conclude with the admission that he had written
the letter as much for himself as for the addressee. He
knew now that he wanted to be a writer and tried to com-
pose essays for publication on a variety of subjects. He
had written a novel about Berkeley, which only his
mother liked, and he was writing another about Munich,
but, except for the editor of his hometown newspaper,
who took some pieces on European sights, no one would
publish any of these. His letters, the expectations for
which could be less grand, supplemented the failed formal
writing as a kind of literary apprenticeship.

Indeed, it is worth noting here that his correspondence served well throughout Steffens's career as a draft-
ing board for more formal writing. Incidents recounted
in letters would appear later in an article or a story.
More often, one suspects, the act of relating an experience
to a correspondent *structured* that experience in the
stream of his current thinking or much later writing. That
is why, though he wrote his *Autobiography* without access to his letters (which were found in a family trunk
after he died), the story of his life is often remarkably
close to the letters in its characterizations of men and
events. He often gave vitality to his letters with extended
dialogues between himself and the many people he met
over a lifetime.

And there would come that time during the First
World War and the Bolshevik Revolution when publishers
were wary of him and he had to turn to his letters as the
primary mode of expression. Immediately before that
time of exclusion, in 1917, he told his youngest sister,

Laura, that "this is not a letter-writing generation. My friend's letters are like mine: brief, careless, never thoughtful, hard, expressive. They are principally appointments to meet and talk, and we do talk." [9] Still, his own, at least, had to improve because for a while these appointments were all he had.

The student letters from Europe were, of course, not as "mature" as some of this later correspondence would be, and many of them were sophomoric in their striving for a maturity the young Steffens simply did not have. In several letters he fancied himself his sisters' mentor, telling his mother once that he wanted to guide their reading from the vantage point of his own new learning. He instructed Louise in a reading of Plato, suggesting that she read his own notebook commentaries as a basic gloss. Another time he was casually distinguishing for her the differences between Ludwig van Beethoven and Richard Wagner when, perhaps suddenly taken with his own erudition, he shifted to a lecture mode: "Let us add another and, thus having a trio, see if we can distinguish the planes of art. I will take Strauss." There followed a facile discussion of the mental states induced by and appealed to by Johann Strauss, Wagner, and Beethoven. His sister Lottie wanted to be a writer, so her unpublished big brother lectured her on the subjects of plot and character.[10]

The content and even the style of a letter depended very much upon the person it was intended for, so that in letters to other correspondents he might turn around and present himself as a student. Even the "life of unlearning" theme appears in a letter he wrote to his father in December 1890. One of the things that sent him to Germany was the search for a reasonable ethics in chaotic modern life. Aware of Joseph Steffens's political activities, and bowing now to him as teacher, he asked whether politics and morality were compatible. Given the realities and temptations of political life, how should a

man of politics govern himself? "It were surely right for
me to know the truth of the matter now," he said, "especially as I shall know some day—perhaps too late to
guide myself accordingly." The letter had an urgent tone
which suggested anxiety over having to wait to *experience* the truth. He was annoyed that others around him
already knew it.[11]

These are essentially matters of style and are important because they prefigure the personae Steffens
would either adopt himself or impose on others as his
writing developed. There are other, more substantive
traits he developed in this period which also helped shape
later writing.

First is his self-conscious adoption of a scientific outlook. The very word "scientific" recurs so often in all his
writing that it takes on the role of a major theme. What
he meant by it was simply that the world and everything
in it could be observed, measured, and catalogued in an
objective manner and that reliable predictions about the
behavior of men and matter could be drawn from that
study. Later he would look for and claim to find the laws
governing social movement and revolution. By the 1920's
he would know in a "scientific" sense why world revolution was inevitable. In these formative European years,
though, he identified few laws. The scientific idea was
itself a satisfying discovery. He knew only that whether
one were a student of politics, an artist, or, as he identified himself now, a *litterateur,* one must search out the
truth from life's hidden, unlovely depths. He would be a
realist. He spoke on behalf of realistic art, for example,
and said he would "go down in the mud to clear a way
for the advance it needs must have. . . ." His own fiction
must be realistic. Near the end of his European tour he
was at work on a novel about the low life of Munich, a
work he knew would be ill-received by a reading public
interested more in fanciful literature than in hard, scientific fact. "But I shall do my best," he told a friend about

his never-finished work, "to find and present some truths and shall surely keep within the limits of facts." [12]

Steffens even subjected himself to the scientific method. On the eve of his secret marriage to Josephine Bontecou, in 1891, he noticed that his sexual desire for her had fallen off. Someone told him he had seen this sort of thing happen in the case of another young man. Steffens, apparently undisturbed by its occurrence in himself, decided that his case was an interesting scientific confirmation of the fact that true love, originating in his higher nature, was overwhelming his baser self. "Thus without taking a thought, the unconscious repugnance to the lower nature caused a cessation of the action of the physical." Then, a bare six months after they were married, he and Josephine found they were drifting apart altogether. The scientist in him tried to explain that, too. He told a friend that "in the midst of our trouble we hit upon the simple method of solution known as analysis, diagnosis, and the result was a comprehension of the disease. . . . We found by means of the application of the scientific method that something was gone,—something which cannot be retained,—and, giving it up, we have since learned that the missing link is not an essential to plain, healthy contentment with reasonable bursts of happiness." [13]

His talk of higher and lower natures suggests another aspect of Steffens's scientific outlook: his attraction to naturalism. This was the social philosophy which nineteenth-century thinkers in virtually every field spun out of the works of Herbert Spencer and Charles Darwin. Spencer's description of physical science and Darwin's of biology taught that matter and life forms were subject to natural laws of formation and development, and that both were constantly evolving into new forms. Naturalism was a revolt against the imprecision and subjectivity of nineteenth-century romanticism, on the one hand, and against the static universe of the eighteenth-century Enlighten-

ment on the other. Within a remarkably short time after
Spencer published *Social Statics* in 1850 and Darwin issued *The Origin of Species* in 1859, theologians, lawyers, psychologists, sociologists, economists and literary
artists were rushing to adapt their work to the new
science. All were in rough agreement that the primacy of
natural law and the evolution of species, institutions, and
ideas were assumptions on which a new examination of
life and society must be based.

Naturalism found adherents among such American
novelists as Theodore Dreiser and Frank Norris. Dreiser's
claim was that the protagonists in *Sister Carrie* (1900)
and *An American Tragedy* (1925) were moved less by
their own wills than by large impersonal forces. Norris's
McTeague (1899) showed that man could evolve through
higher and higher levels of civilization, but that his civilized state would be only a cover for the residual brutality
of his origins that always lurked close beneath the
surface.

Steffens was interested in thinking about higher and
lower natures, too. In addition to observations of himself,
he commented on the behavior of others. Speculating on
the conduct of men in the business world, he wrote this to
a friend:

Tell me honestly and soberly, don't you see that most men
have not the light of the man, that they are not much above
animals? The whole business world acts by instinct. Their
very self-restraint (not even that is often apparent) comes
not from the morality of the thinking mind, but from the
habit or instinct, more or less strongly born in them.[14]

When he wrote these lines, Steffens had been wondering for some time whether men were capable of moral
behavior. The *Autobiography* organizes almost the whole
European tour around this theme. That was something of a
distortion, but it was nonetheless a persistent intellectual
problem. Before he could know if correct conduct were

possible, of course, he had to find out what "correct" meant, and had, therefore, to study ethics. Could there be a firm, unalterable foundation for ethical behavior? Steffens listened to philosophers at the University of Berlin and found them wanting. Could science establish the foundation? He decided it could, if only in a rough way. Naturalistic references to man's lower nature or his residual animal instincts might at least help explain why men behaved the way they did. But the question was how *ought* they to behave? Naturalism helped there, too. If one understood society and the world to be evolving and saw that growth was worthy and inevitable, he decided by the time he returned to America, then any action which hindered growth was bad and any that eased its way was good. Here was a "philosophy" too vague and ill-defined to live by, but it was a start. And it meant that Steffens had rejected any metaphysical backing for ethics in favor of a scientific one.

The scientific outlook was a gradual development in his thinking. He often seemed just as much an idealist, the second intellectual theme of these years, which meant that he thought mind and spiritual values were the only reality. Material things and processes were less important than his own inner contemplation of them. He had no disciplined thoughts on idealism vs. materialism—mind against matter—however, and a reading of his letters suggests that his adherence to idealism was more a loyalty to an old college classmate, Fred Willis, with whom he corresponded irregularly, but at length, than anything else. Willis was deeply, if fuzzily, idealistic and wrote Steffens letters filled with long metaphysical wonderings. Steffens replied as best he could with flowery letters of his own, like this one dated December 8, 1889:

Dear Fred:
    Your letter of the 17th came yesterday morning, and like the calm pure snow which I see out of my window falling

so quietly, it gave, without jar or violence, a new aspect to things about me. Snow is, of course, a novel sight to my eyes, and I find a beautiful pleasure in watching it. The little spirit flakes move past before one with so much dignity, with no sign of haste, with no apparent consciousness that they are going to alight, turning hither and thither in their wanderings, sometimes even stopping to peep through my window and perhaps to come down on the sill,—all with so much calm and yet so much surety of purpose, that their movement moves me only to meditation. But they are not too sober and serious. Now and then you see one stop and coquet with a companion flake, only to dart off in a new direction chased by the other,—perhaps angry after thus being trifled with. If you look out into space so as to get a general view of a few thousands or millions of them your head will bow in sympathy with the slow, but inevitable fall. . . .[15]

Steffens's science would have to cut through this sort of thing before it could be of use to him intellectually. Idealism, linked so closely to his friendship with Willis and Willis's longing for a life of quiet contemplation, did not seem, in the end, to pose much opposition. Steffens read Georg Wilhelm Friedrich Hegel, the most influential of the philosophical idealists, but within a few months of his own arrival in Germany, he was gently suggesting to Willis that he was not as secure in his philosophy as before. Soon he would have to say that he had all but given it up in favor of empirical science. If, even so, he complained to Willis and others that his scientific work with, say, Wilhelm Wundt's psychological apparatus was creeping and tedious, that complaint bespoke not a discontent with scientific thinking but rather a personal chafing at the narrowness of the work he had to do in a laboratory. Steffens wanted breadth, not depth.

He told Willis about this desire for a broad application of the scientific attitude in the form of a general challenge. The letter, written in 1892, a few months before he sailed for New York, said he wanted to immerse himself in the hustle of active life without caring yet where it would take him. "I may answer better when I have sung myself in the streets and heard the sound. I say in the streets. A philosophy, a literature, art,—they must be able to run a railroad, govern a town, a nation, manage a newspaper and sell goods; or they and what they would conduct are wrong. . . ." [16]

The transition from idealism to scientific thinking does not appear to have been either difficult or complete. Perhaps that was because the two were not wholly incompatible. Steffens's professor for the history of philosophy at Heidelberg was Kuno Fischer, a disciple of Hegel who spent a career lecturing with legendary clarity on a variety of philosophies and, more importantly for Steffens, attempting to reconcile Hegel's idealism with the naturalistic theory of evolution. Hegel, after all, argued for progress in dialectical terms—a thesis and its contradiction producing a new, better thesis. Fischer saw something like that happening in the concept of evolution.[17] It is hard to know whether any of this filtered down to Steffens. In any case he would be more scientist than idealist by the time he returned to the United States, but his future writing would always bear the mark of his having been through both.

If the European experience gave him a way of looking at things, it also gave him something to look at: cities. Steffens's experience of European cities created a third element in his thinking. On arriving in Europe he became a conscious urban man. His letters are filled with talk of hotels, boarding houses, beer gardens, restaurants, railroad terminals, markets and libraries. Certainly he had seen these institutions in Sacramento and San Francisco, but what was new was his long, independent experience of them. He liked urban characters, too, and thought about what brought people to the city, whether they hurried or not through its streets and why, and what types among them were likely to be governors of the city and what types were the governed.

"We were at once filled with this spirit of this city,"
the idealist in him could say of Hamburg. But he was also
impressed with physical attributes. He liked the cleanli-
ness and order of German cities, an expression, he assumed, of the fact that they were well-governed, well-
policed. "They say New Yorkers never know how filthy
their streets are until they get back from a tour through
Europe," he wrote in another letter, "and I suppose
that applies to most of our cities. . . . Just think, they
wash or sweep perfectly clean, even to a polish, the
streets." On the other hand, he disliked the gaiety and
glitter of Paris, an expression of Parisian "gilded vice."
Hamburgers, he said, pushed their business and factory
buildings physically to the background of their city's life,
showing that they cared more for aesthetics than work.[18]

Perhaps the best city "essay" he wrote was a com-
parison of Munich with Vienna, which unites his eye for
material data with a more idealistic sense of what it all
means:

A man should always, I think, go to Vienna from Munich, as
I did.

Munich is very typically German—slow, artistic, phleg-
matic, a city of breweries and art schools, where the people
dress utterly without taste, have large feet and don't like to
wear anything but an ugly shoe and a large one. Now land
in the evening in Vienna; there is a rush and a hurry,
laughter and merriment, movement and dash. From the depot
to my hotel was an hour's walk, but I did it slowly and kept
my eyes open. It was a change which set my Germanized
blood boiling. It made me feel as if I wanted some fun,—
even if the cost were considerable loss of self-respect. I held
in, however, and enjoyed seeing the Vienners and Viennerins
enjoy themselves. The women were well-dressed, nicely,
neatly shaped, and looked as full of health as of fun. The
men were gay, not handsome, but manly, not, like a German,
proud and dignified,—but proud, not at all afraid of losing
the dignity which was all comfortable in their hearts, as I
found out afterwards.

Well, I spent two weeks in Vienna. Vienna produces the finest medical men in the world,—but no art, no philosophy, no music, no literature. Why? Because the depths are rotten with disease and filth,—from which the doctors get their practise,—and the upper regions are secondary to the depths. The demi-monde leads the life of Vienna as it does the styles of Europe, and demi-anything produces nothing. The world gains in one way from all this badness—the hospital of about 10 acres of beds is full and the diseases are of all kinds and once in the hospital a man, a woman, becomes a subject and ceases to be human. It is awful—it may be scientific,—but it is vile, and students may educate their hands, eyes, and brain here, but heart, soul, all that is gentleman, sensitive, must be dulled. . . .[19]

Is this letter idealistic or materialistic? Does some overall Viennese consciousness produce "a rush and a hurry, laughter and merriment, movement and dash"? Or is it that the material environment—"the depths . . . rotten with disease and filth"—produces science and a dulled sensitivity? Clearly, the answer must be both. Steffens was not a disciplined thinker and had, really, no need to be. When he left Europe for America in 1892 he carried with him an interest in cities and their politics and an interest in thinking about everything in whatever manner seemed to suit the occasion.

He was twenty-six years old when he came back, married, unemployed, and "educated." He had grown up in an atmosphere of middle class security, and he had spent years as a student in formal institutions. He would be grateful for the security, but, increasingly, Steffens grew resentful at the fraud the schools had perpetrated on him. He would have to work hard now, he thought, to erase their myths and replace them with truer pictures. He would become figuratively a student of American urban life, immigration and politics. What he learned—or "unlearned"—he would teach through the new medium of mass circulation journalism.

The letter from his father which a messenger handed Steffens when his ship landed at New York gave a partial summary of his education and also pointed in a new direction. Steffens "quoted" it from memory in his autobiobraphy, but its brief, staccato sentences could just as well be his:

My dear son:

When you finished school you wanted to go to college. I sent you to Berkeley. When you got through there, you did not care to go into my business; so I sold out. You preferred to continue your studies in Berlin. I let you. After Berlin it was Heidelberg; after that Leipzig. And after the German universities you wanted to study at the French universities in Paris. I consented, and after a year with the French, you had to have half a year of the British Museum in London. All right. You had that too.

By now you must know about all there is to know of the theory of life, but there's a practical side as well. It's worth knowing. I suggest that you learn it, and the way to study it, I think, is to stay in New York and hustle.

Enclosed please find one hundred dollars, which should keep you till you can find a job and support yourself.[20]

2

●●

Reporter

Young men who wanted to write in the 1890s could find no better school for their craft than the city room of a big metropolitan newspaper. David Graham Phillips, himself a newspaperman and novelist, said that "the daily newspaper sustains the same relation to a young writer as the hospital to the medical student. It is the first great school of practical experience." [1] Politics, money, crime, violence and sheer humanity filled newspaper columns every day. They got there because reporters hunted them, found them, and put them there. The reporters who wanted "practical experience" to feed their literary aspirations found it in abundance. Theodore Dreiser, Stephen Crane, Harold Frederic, Abraham Cahan, and Eugene Field were among the writers whose preparation included work in journalism.

Lincoln Steffens began with newspapers, too. From 1892 to 1897 he reported news for the *New York Evening Post*, and from 1897 to 1901 he edited the city department of the *New York Commercial Advertiser*. Together with other reporter-writers he sometimes worried that the narrow sort of writing newspapers required would kill his budding literary career. As Larzer Ziff has noted, a newspaper was as often a cemetery as it was a school. But gradually Steffens relaxed as he saw that he could create an unusual career between the news and literature by combining the best of reportorial journalism with his real skill at literary characterization. [2]

Almost all Steffens's writing in the 1890s derived
from his newspaper work. The single interesting excep-
tion is a story called "Sweet Punch" which *Harper's* published in December 1893. He wrote it over a winter week-
end some months after arriving in New York. *Harper's*
gave him $30 for it, but more important than the money
was the heady feeling that came of having won his way
early into one of the country's most prestigious magazines. "Last night," he wrote to his father when he had
the check in hand, "I scored my first purely literary
success." [3]

"Sweet Punch" is about a successful businessman
who finds himself reflecting back on the principles and
ideals he learned and debated in college. On Christmas
Eve his imagination recreates a discussion among class-
mates which took place during another holiday season.
He and his friends pledged themselves then to conduct
their future business dealings on the highest ethical plane.
Now he sees that he has abandoned that pledge, made a
great deal of money, and ruined one of the men who sat
with him on that other Christmas Eve.

Clearly, the story is a speculative projection of his
own career. It was written in haste but bears a close relationship to Steffens's doubts, extending back over several years, about the possibility of right conduct. The
story could not yet be based upon his personal observation of businessmen. Instead it draws on his own autobiographical guess about ethics and ambition. The first-
person narrator gently blames his wife for driving him
into unchecked materialism, suggesting, perhaps, a role
for his own wife, Josephine. And Steffens's father and the
schools he sent him to are the subjects of this elaboration of the "unlearning" theme:

As for the world [he thought once, naively], it was peopled
by men who erred sometimes in a vague way, but in general
appeared as our fathers did at home. We never doubted that
honesty, industry, thrift, and such simple virtues would make

us as successful careers as any men could run. So it looked
then—in college days. Strange how different the world is
from what it seems to students' eyes! [4]

An innocent made newly aware, he now regrets he ever
learned about the "purer life."

It is an interesting curiosity that about the time he
wrote "Sweet Punch" Steffens was also writing increasingly strident, unregretful letters to his college friend
Fred Willis concerning his busy, materialistic life in New
York. Philosophy was for children and old men, he hinted
in one letter, and he spoke of "the joy I feel on finding
myself an active sharer, a busy part, of the noisy, hurried, over-serious life about me in New York. I enjoy this
American living, working and running, and I admire this
healthy American manhood." [5] Probably the letters were
no more representative of him than the story. Steffens
owned the sentiments expressed in both. Together they
show simply that he was not settled, not comfortable yet
with what he was doing.

The *New York Evening Post*
and "Human Interest" Stories

The money "Sweet Punch" brought was the only
money he earned in these first few months. Otherwise, he
lived on his mother-in-law's generosity, searching every
day for a job but reluctant to use his father's connections
to find one. Finally he gave in and, armed with a letter
from someone his father knew, went to see Robert Underwood Johnson of the *Century Magazine*. Johnson sized
him up and sent him to the *New York Evening Post*.

The *Post* was among the oldest and most respectable
newspapers in New York. Alexander Hamilton founded
it in 1801, and William Cullen Bryant edited it with bril-
liance for half a century after 1829. By the time Steffens
arrived it was under the firm, very conservative hand of

Edwin Lawrence Godkin.[6] A man of striking appearance, with his bushy beard and mustache, Godkin was
rarely seen in his newspaper's offices by any but the top
editors. Steffens recalled receiving a polite nod from him
once, but Godkin so isolated himself from the lower levels
that it was said he could ride up the elevator with his top
reporters and not recognize their faces. He rarely read
beyond the *Post*'s front page and editorials, and the careful crafting of the latter occupied most of his attention on
any given day.

Yet his will guided even the smallest department.
The *Post* was Godkin's paper absolutely. Steffens spoke
for the entire staff when he said that his function as a
reporter was to be "legs" for Godkin. And since in his
idle hours Steffens read nothing but the *Post*, Godkin was
"mind" to him. The paper was a tightly integrated or-
ganic unity, its separate functions ordered from the top.
Godkin was a financial conservative, so the *Post* was Wall
Street's unofficial spokesman. Godkin hated New York's
succession of corrupt, Tammany governments, so the *Post*
stood for good men in good government (the "goo-goo's,"
his opponents called them).

Godkin was also a man of considerable refinement
and education, and he imposed upon the *Post* a journal-
istic style which appealed to gentlemen like himself.
Steffens did not mind the paper's politics or its economics;
indeed, Robert Underwood Johnson sent him to the *Post*
because he thought with his current leanings he would be
happy there. But the dull, weightiness of the *Post*'s style
was more than oppressive. Steffens would complain long
afterward that Godkin's demands left his writing permanently impaired.[7] Godkin's argument was that the mindless stylistic simplicities of his sensational rivals, Charles
A. Dana's *New York Sun* and Joseph Pulitzer's *New York
World*, for example, permanently damaged their readers'
sensibilities. People who were used to only the most rudi-

mentary, facile sentence constructions could never again think on any but a rudimentary, facile level.

In any case, Steffens soon discovered for himself another value of the *Post*'s dullness. The 1890s was a depression decade. The Panic of 1893 broke out the very winter Steffens came to work, and his early assignments included financial reporting from Wall Street. Soon he noticed that financial men liked to give out the first news of bank failures and other troubles to the *Post*, not just because they knew Godkin would be sympathetic on the editorial page but because they knew such news would be broken in a dull, protective, matter-of-fact rhetoric that would reduce its impact.[8]

However damaging he may have remembered it, the writing Steffens did for the *Post* between 1892 and 1897, when read again today, shows him learning and making the most of his reportorial assignments. True, he wrote dull financial news and many commonplace stories. But he also wrote literate reviews of New York's active German theater as well as dramatic accounts of news events. When the seventeen-story Ireland Building collapsed, Norman Hapgood, a colleague, recalled that Steffens was able in a few minutes to dictate an extensive, orderly, expert account that also caught in its prose the suddenness and significance of the disaster. On the other hand, Steffens once wrote a sensational story about a music teacher who died under distressing circumstances. The city editor put it on the front page where Godkin saw it, and the story nearly cost Steffens his job.[9]

Fortunately, he found a middle way. He was aided by Godkin's fight against political corruption. Widespread allegations concerning bribery and vice in the New York City police department led the *Post*, by 1894, to join the Rev. Charles Parkhurst in a much-publicized crusade. The state legislature at Albany created the Lexow Committee, named for Clarence Lexow, its chairman, and soon

the *Post* was in the thick of a major reform effort.
Steffens's immediate superior, City Editor Henry J.
Wright, sent him on regular assignments to the Mulberry
Street Police Station to investigate and report what he
could. The *Post* had never reported "police news" before
and, unlike the more sensational papers, never had an
office on Mulberry Street, so Steffens's work there was
something new for the paper and its reporter.

With loyalty to his newspaper and enthusiasm of his
own, Steffens attacked politicians and policemen in the
pages of the *Post*. Much later he would recreate these experiences with impressive (and probably imaginative)
detail when he wrote his *Autobiography*. But, as far as
the development of his writing was concerned, he did
something of equal importance: he discovered for himself the "human interest story." Spreading out for blocks
below the Mulberry Street Station was a vast immigrant
ghetto peopled with Irishmen, Italians, Germans, Jews
from Eastern Europe, and Chinese from across the Pacific.
These people, their poverty, their meanness, their virtue,
their attempts to preserve old world cultures while their
children adapted to the new, were for Steffens a new
and fascinating subject. As his contacts with them grew,
so did his sympathies. He found himself going among
them as much for his own interest as to try to get stories
about them into the *Post*.

What he did write about them were human interest
stories. This form, which Steffens certainly did not invent,
has a history and a self-conscious structure which makes
it eligible for consideration as a literary genre in its own
right.[10]

A human interest story is not news in the conven-
tional sense. It is a report of a current happening, but it
is not absolutely up-to-date and it does not go "stale" over–
night. The subjects of human interest stories are endless,
but often they involve major occurrences in the lives of
common people or, perhaps, hidden, obscure aspects of

public people's lives. Great poverty or great wealth have been favorite topics. Thus, the *New York Times*'s annual series on "New York's One Hundred Neediest Cases," which has been published as a spur to Christmas charity for years, is a human interest collection; so are tales of the private life—and death—of the fabulously wealthy Howard Hughes. Death is a typical subject, involving sometimes the passionate death of murder, or the careless, accidental deaths of ghetto children.

What further distinguishes a human interest story from straight news is that each has a discrete focus of attention. A front-page news story focuses simply and immediately on the central event being reported: the collapse of a coal mine, the resignation of a government official, the meeting and transactions of a local school board. The essential news is given in the economical wording of the opening paragraph.

A human interest story, on the other hand, is apt to be more leisurely, and also more suspenseful. But beyond that, the story focuses less on a central event than on human reaction to the event. If the story is about a tenement fire, for example, the precise address, the number of engines responding to the call and the dollar value of the loss are not so important as where, say, a particular named family was when the fire broke out, which members perished and how, what cherished possessions were burned, what heroism or venality the fire produced. In short, a human interest story aims to make public the normally private social facts that something like a fire makes suddenly visible.

The most essential ingredient in a good human-interest story, however, is probably the reporter himself. In Steffens's time reporters in this genre saw themselves as writers of popular literature and insisted on their own artistry. Their work dealt with specific events occurring at specific times, but their use of the news aimed at demonstrating what was universal in it. That was why their human interest stories were timely without being time-bound. They did not fabricate events, but they did select and order them in an attempt to reveal truths about life or human character. Sometimes reporters made their judgments explicit, but more often they allowed actions and events to stand as symbols, implying rather than stating the writer's vision. His intent might have been little more than to offer a "slice of life," but the reporter's personal rendering of it insured that the story carried as much of his own character as of the people he wrote about.

A few human interest stories are good enough to extricate themselves from their news value and become timeless. Theodore Dreiser's classic *An American Tragedy* (1925) is often said to be a kind of grand-scale human interest story, so closely did Dreiser, a newspaper man, draw and even copy its details from an actual murder case. Still, if not all stories can live forever, a succession of them can do the next best thing: provide a continuous flow of stories for steady newspaper readers. Since the character and often the structure of human interest stories are much alike, each single story need only beguile the reader for a day or so before it is replaced by another of equal value. Thus, the genre rather than the single story becomes the satisfying, looked-for reading experience. This is a pattern peculiar to journalism because it takes advantage of the fact that newspapers are themselves constantly perishing, constantly regenerating formats of expression.

Ever since the appearance of human-interest journalism in the 1830's, the temptation to mere sensationalism had been strong. The lurid accounts of fire and murder in James Gordon Bennett's *New York Herald* after 1835 and, more recently, Pulitzer's *World* in the 1890s made those papers panderers as well as reporters.

Lincoln Steffens's newspaper writing was never sensational. Godkin, of course, would not have stood for it, and Steffens himself would not have wanted to invest the news with any more excitement than its substance warranted. A tone of understatement, not extravagance, characterizes his newspaper writing. But he did use human interest techniques in almost everything he wrote about immigrants, politicians, and common people. Here, for example, is a story he wrote for the October 24, 1896 edition of the *Post*. It might have been a commonplace report, but Steffens's literary sense gave it special shape. It was headed "A Frenzied Italian" and may be given in full:

A 'longshoreman, Reiley by name, was walking along Chatham Square at 4:30 o'clock this morning, when his pipe went out. He asked the man ahead of him for a match. The answer was two sharp, stinging blows, one in the chest, the other on the arm. In a daze he turned to a policeman nearby and said:

"Officer, that man hit me, and it hurts like ———."

Patrolman Lockwood, the officer, saw that the 'longshoreman was bleeding, and he ran after the assailant. Before he reached him the fellow had attacked a German who was absorbed in a study of the bill of fare board of a restaurant.

"Poletzei, poletzei," shrieked the German. Lockwood came up and saw that the man with the knife was an Italian. But the Italian saw him at the same moment and attacked the officer with his weapon, an oyster-knife. The two began fencing, the officer using his club. The Italian was very skillful and kept Lockwood off till a lodger coming down the stairs of a hotel behind him distracted the attention of the Italian, who, throwing his knife at the policeman, turned to meet the supposed attack from the rear. Then Lockwood closed, and another policeman arriving, they dragged the prisoner struggling like a madman to the station-house. He said he was Giuseppe Borrelli. His victims were cared for by an ambulance surgeon.

Borrelli was arraigned before Magistrate Simms in Center Street Court this morning and held in $1,000 bail for trial on the charge of felonious assault, but the Magistrate

recommended to the District Attorney's office that a commission be appointed to inquire into the man's sanity. Reilly
and the German were both sent to the House of Detention to
await the action of the District Attorney, who has been
urged to make all possible haste in the matter.[11]

The story does not begin with a standard opening-
paragraph summary, because Steffens was unconcerned
with the event as news to be read and "known" quickly.
It was instead a story to be told. The story's purpose is to
demonstrate the flow of ongoing action through the lives
of six people. The six—Reiley, the Italian, the German,
two policemen, and the lodger—were unrelated until
Borrelli's mad attacks—and Steffens's rendering of them
—bring them together. The story is not, then, about an
event that happened but rather about an event *happening*. The first focus of attention is on Reiley, in need of a
light and unaware of the role he is about to play. The
Italian stabs him but then flees. Steffens's story leaves
Reiley and follows the attacker, developing as the events
themselves do. The policeman did not know he would ap-
prehend the assailant until he actually did it, and the
reader does not know either until he does it in Steffens's
story. The reader does not even know the Italian's name
until he says himself that he is Giuseppe Borrelli.

This is hardly the stuff of classic literature. But it
is a nicely restrained use of the human interest technique
of reporting a news event as a series of live interactions.
The telling of the tale must approximate the experiencing
of the events.

One of the best ways to do that, of course, was for
the reporter to write himself into his work by making the
story of his own visits and interviews the substance and
structure of his piece. The news of an event is then
matched with the "news" of the reporter's investigation.
Both are reported in an integrated story. Steffens adopted
this motif often. Once in 1894 he wrote a standard news
story about corruption in the police department and the

Board of Police Commissioners' slowness in dealing with
it. A few days later he reported as a news event in itself
his own visit to the office of J. J. Martin, President of the
Board, for a comment on the story. Martin swore at
him and called an officer to throw him out. Steffens wrote
up their dialogue and headlined it "J. J. Martin's Irritability." [12]

Another story, about labor conflicts on the Jewish
Lower East Side, begins with Steffens himself watching an
Italian woman, "young, lithe, and proud . . . a gay spot
of color on the dark gray of the ghetto," walking among
Jews on Hester Street. The reporter sees the men scowl at
her and hears the women jeer at her in Yiddish. He is
puzzled and asks a Jewish labor leader standing nearby
the cause of such a response.

"What is it," asked the reporter, "makes your women hate
her so; is it racial or only sexual?"
    "It isn't either," he said. "It's industrial. They don't
see the woman or her fine clothes, but the bundle on her
head."

The reporter looks again and sees a bundle of newly
made men's trousers balanced on the Italian woman's
head. He realizes—and now so does the reader—that she
symbolizes the invasion of the Jewish garment industry by
Italian newcomers.[13]

In this story Steffens poses as an idle bystander whose
attention is caught first by the demeanor and color of a
woman crossing Hester Street. The rest of the story un-
folds from there. But in another story, "New York Shop
Girls," he makes his own more deliberate investigation of
an attempted suicide the opening attraction:

A white girl took Paris green in Little Africa the other day.
It did not matter much, especially since she has recovered.
There were a number of other white girls in the same street
who did not take poison, and that matters a great deal;
they are at the very bottom of society, and are utterly beyond

recovery. The policeman who reported the case of the attempted suicide said there was no story in it; he explained
that he thought maybe there was because he heard the girl
came from a rich family, but she only came out of the
tenements, so "there wasn't nothing into it." The fat negro
woman who came sloppily down the stairs to the basement
door to answer the reporter's knock was of a mind with the
policeman.

"I jes' guess ye can't write her up, honey. She's no good
an' dat's all yer can make out o' it. You's jes' had yer walk
fer nuffin' 'tall."

"Didn't you ever hear her say where she came from or
what she was?"

"Not a syllabum."

"Never a syllable about a husband either?"

"Oh, yes, a husband, in course; dey all hez a husband
befo', dese white gals hez, shoar."

"Ever say anything about working somewhere?"

"Nope, nuffin' 'tall. Oh, yes, you mind me how one day
I and her wuz washing by de pump in de backyard 'n' she
says sumpfin 'bout buttons."

Buttons; that was the story, and so old that no further
inquiries were necessary.[14]

Why? Because the girl was a button-sewer in a garment
shop, and she reminds him of all the shop girls in the city.
Now he casts off the role of puzzled investigator and assumes that of wise commentator. The story concludes with
the reporter's rueful, imaginative speculation about the
life cycle of these young women. Lives of boredom spawn
dreams of fulfillment in marriage, but the wedding is
succeeded by dream-crushing drudgery. If they have
babies they can survive by devotion to their children; if
not, they end up in the police court or swallow "Paris
green."

Clearly, interviewing was not just a task associated
with Steffens's new profession, not just a means to the
end of accurate news reporting. The interviewer was, for

Steffens, a kind of literary persona, a way he chose to see himself. His human interest stories were still centered on interesting characters and on the flow of life which their interactions produced, but his personal discovery of their lives was often a subject in itself. The interviews, and more importantly his reports of them as dialogues, were a further development of Steffens's student pose. He sees clearly, but he is often innocent and unaware of his observations' significance. He talks to people, asks questions, and learns. Thus, he sees the Italian woman jeered on Hester Street but has to ask why. And, even if much of "New York Shop Girls" is a sociological essay on the shop girl "type," Steffens cannot really begin until he has interviewed the black woman and heard her give him the magic word: "buttons."

Steffens did not write about these stories in his autobiography, but he remembered or imagined numerous other interviews. From the vantage point of a man sixty years old he sometimes portrayed himself as a naive boy-reporter whom businessmen and politicians must enlighten. Elsewhere the *Autobiography* portrays him as a wily, bluffing interrogator who, given ten minutes, could get anybody to reveal his innermost secrets. Neither character embodied the truth. He was neither as innocent nor as clever as he imagined in alternate moods. But Steffens liked interviewing, was good at it, and, as is clear from his *Post* stories, made it an early mainstay of his literary career.

Some of Steffens's best human-interest writing was in the "slice of life" mode. The object, again, was to write less about a particular event than about what an event revealed concerning the condition of life. A good example is this brief notice headlined "A Small Babel at a Fire":

Fire, one of the five original elements of nature, united in one common fear all the mixed human elements of a Hester

Street tenement-house at 10:15 o'clock today. "Fuoco!
Fuoco!" was the first cry. It came in a shrill shriek from
Cornelia Palermo, an Italian streetcleaner's wife, on the
fifth and top floor of no. 44. Other voices, other tongues took
it up on the successive floors. "Feuer! Feuer! es brennt
oben!" was the German woman's alarm. "Waih geschrieggen!
es brennt!" wailed the Polish girl on the second floor. "Fi-er!
Fi-er!" Carl Weiss put it in "der English." [15]

Here Steffens imagines the immigrant ghetto a mixture of
atomized lives, sharing nothing. Then the fire, "an element of nature," suddenly unites them. They shout their
successive discoveries as the fire rushes from the top floor
to the street. Yet at the very moment it forces them to
share its terrors, the fire also reveals and heightens their
separateness. The fire "happens" in this paragraph, but
so also does the revelation of the immigrants' brief unity
and its ironic contradiction.

Steffens used the technique of placing disparate
events in ironic juxtaposition for another piece headlined "A Bird Dealer's Loss." It is ostensibly a report
concerning a pet shop's destruction by fire, but the
story's subtitle, "Succession of Sensations in Little Hungary," points to its larger subject. The first paragraph offers some basic, almost standard, information, but at the
same time it deliberately withholds enough to force the
reader to read on and explore the story's opening ironies:

Old Hans Bodd's birds and animals were nearly all burned
or smothered to death this morning. He wept bitter tears,
and Essex Street near Houston, where his little shop was,
filled with his neighbors who sorrowed with him. They did
not buy of his stock, but they had loved to watch him feed,
clean, and caress his pets. But after a while the other bird
man over in Houston Street let his monkey loose, and everybody turned to laugh at Jocko's antics till the barber's baby
was run over. When that occurred horror and shrieks succeeded the amusement and laughter that had followed sorrow
and tears, and then there was nothing left to "Little Hungary" but work.[16]

The story that follows is simply an elaboration on these themes: Steffens invests each character, including the charming, thieving monkey, with a history and a personality and casts the whole in human interest dialogue. Still, the main theme is not the separate events but the "succession of sensations" from tragedy to laughter and from fear to resignation. What the events reveal, then, is their own sheer variety and the rapid variation in the social moods they generate.

The ambience of immigrant neighborhoods like "Little Hungary" fascinated Steffens. He wrote about immigrants often and even the least of his accounts tries to capture the essential motion and flux in their lives. He seemed especially aware that their condition was never static but shifted and evolved in a constant adjustment and readjustment to their surroundings. He wrote about two things in particular that always threatened their stability: the often explosive mixing of immigrant groups and the uneasy relations between the first and second generations within a given nationality.

The problem of mixing came from the fact that New York did not really have one immigrant ghetto but rather a collection of distinct neighborhoods, each generally dominated by one or another nationality. Irishmen, Italians, Germans, Chinese and others were territorial. But at the same time they were continually expanding or impinging upon each other, and individual residents might attempt to cross the invisible lines which otherwise separated them. Steffens thought he saw a general pattern, for example, when he observed the Italian garment worker walk colorfully through the Jewish section with a bundle of trousers on her head. She was crossing a territorial and an industrial boundary at the same time. A supposed Italian invasion of Harlem was the similar subject of "Race War in Harlem." The displaced natives, Irishmen, and blacks captured most of Steffens's sympathy in this report. He described a "battle line" at 115th Street

but portrayed a generally quiet struggle in which the most
dramatic weapon was a pile of garbage dumped in the
enemy's backyard.[17]

Not all these conflicts were hostile, and neither was
Steffens's attitude always sympathetic. Most often he
found cultural mixing poignant. "Bloke Murray's Golden
Moon" is an example. Published in 1897 after he left the
New York Post, it was a piece of fiction which reflected
his observations during these earlier years. Bloke Murray,
a native, perhaps, falls in love with a beautiful Chinese
girl and tries to buy her, according to what he (and
Steffens) imagines is the Oriental custom. The girl is de-
lighted with Murray, but she is already married. Her
Chinese husband pretends to negotiate while he lulls
Murray into a stupor with opium. When he awakens,
Murray discovers that his love, Golden Moon, has meanwhile been sold to a Boston laundryman. Murray's love
for the childlike girl is truly touching, and Steffens does
passably with his character. But the Chinese characters
are hardly above popular stereotypes: the girl is a porce-
lain figure and her husband is just another inscrutable,
scheming opium-eater, long familiar to the frightened
xenophobic American imagination.[18]

Steffens did better with his studies of Lower East Side
Jews. For a time in the mid-1890s he was an active pro-
moter of Jewish culture; he fasted and attended syna-
gogue services and even nailed a mezuzah in his office
doorway. The human interest reporting and fiction he
wrote about Jews were deeply sensitive to the meaning of
the High Holy Days and Jewish customs. But one aspect
of their lives especially caught his attention: the erosion
of sympathy between the first and second generations.
Immigrants and their children came into conflict when
attraction to American values and mores grew incompatible with old-world Jewish culture. Steffens was hardly the
first to notice this generational conflict, any more than he

was first to report the larger conflict between national-
ities. But he invested his observation with a heartfelt—
if also sentimental—sympathy, usually in favor of those
who wanted to preserve the old ways.

In "Schloma, Daughter of Schmuhl," for example, a
short story he published in *Chap-Book*, Steffens wrote
about the daughter of a Jewish garment sewer. She works
dutifully all day in her father's business, but the neigh-
borhood community fears she is disloyal to him and to her
heritage. She cannot help but sing while she works, often
the street songs her father hates. "Let her labor be long
and be silent," the community says, "that her son's sons
may sing songs." The temptations become stronger and
the injunctions less subtle. One day she walks alone in the
streets:

It was Essex Street, near Grand. The crowd and the darkness
were comforting to the harrassed girl, who stood there still
now and dizzy in the human stream. Around her flowed the
tired shop-workers, a sluggish, serious tide, which sparkled
here and there with the merry troops of youthful idlers out
for fun.

Suddenly her ear catches the worst insult: "Schickse,
Schickse—Nafke! Pfui!" (gentile, gentile—whore!). And
it serves only to drive her into the arms of the next group
of merry-makers she meets. At home, waiting late for her
to return, her father weeps. The story itself distributes
sympathy about evenly between the girl and her father.
But Steffens weighted the matter somewhat differently
when he described the piece to a friend. It was "founded
on a fact of observation," he said, "and means to tell why,
if not indifferently to justify, the way many of our East
Side Jewish girls are going to the bad." The story is not
worth much as sociology: Steffens's friend and fellow
newspaperman Abraham Cahan certainly got much closer
to explaining not only what the attraction of "America"

was but also *how* it drew younger immigrants away from
their own tradition.* But Steffens could see, at least, that
the conflict was there and that it had a certain blameless
inevitability.[19]

His sympathy for Jewish immigrants in general is
worth noting, because, obviously, not all writers shared it.
Even the great Jacob Riis, who worked for the *New York
Sun* and helped Steffens get a start on his Mulberry
Street beat, did not have much respect for Jews. His
famous book *How the Other Half Lives* (1890) was a
plea for understanding concerning poor aliens, but it
had two chapters on the East Side which suggested that
the persecution of Jews in the old world and the new
was something they brought on themselves by their own
mean behavior. Steffens could hardly agree because, as
he would put it later, "I at that time was almost a Jew."
He was close enough to know better.[20]

Editing the *Commercial Advertiser*

In 1897 Steffens and some other members of the *Post*
staff moved to the *New York Commercial Advertiser*. It
was a dull sheet with a moribund circulation, but Steffens
took over as City Editor and, with the others, hoped to
use the lessons he had learned writing for the *Post* to
breathe new life into it. At least one commentator was
doubtful, however; Steffens clipped this newspaper note
for his scrapbook:

The Commercial Advertiser, the good old grandmother of
journalism, is still being printed.
        Why, God only knows.

---

* Cahan's *Yekl* (1896) explored the conflict between an American-
ized Jewish immigrant and his more recently arrived wife. In 1898
Cahan published *The Imported Bridegroom and Other Stories from
the Jewish Ghetto* and, in 1917, his masterpiece, *The Rise of David
Levinsky.*

A Mr. Steffens is the city editor. He wears on his chin a little downy fuzz he thinks is a beard and he gets $25 a week. That is all I know about him, except that he used to be on the Evening Post and once had a story printed in the Chap Book.[21]

Steffens was not to be put off. He gathered around him a staff consisting of as few professional reporters as possible. He wanted writers, not reporters, believing that a metropolitan daily could indeed be a school for men with literary ambition and, further, that the newspaper itself would improve the more such literary men it had. Within a few months Steffens hired Robert Dunn, Hutchins Hapgood, who would later write the classic *Spirit of the Ghetto* (1902), and Abraham Cahan, whose *Yekl* and other ghetto fiction Steffens admired and whom he promptly sent to his own old Mulberry Street beat. Soon there were only two "reporters" left and these Steffens expected to replace when the writers learned their work. Steffens had seen enough of reporters scrambling for news beats on his old downtown assignments. Now he instructed his young college graduates that they must beat their rivals on how they *presented* the news. He told them what he also told his father: that his paper must have "literary charm as well as daily information, mood as well as sense, gayety as well as seriousness." He would impose no *Commercial Advertiser* style as there was a *Post* style or a *Sun* style. Each writer must work to develop his own way of presenting the news. He would be satisfied if they kept its human side in mind. If a man has murdered his wife, the first question should be *why?* Why does a man kill his wife? What happens between the wedding and the murder? Write, he remembered telling his staff, so that the reader will not merely want to see the man hanged.[22]

Steffens liked to think this policy was successful. The paper's columns did brighten up, and William Dean Howells said that now no writer could afford to miss reading it. In the city room Steffens led or listened to debates on art, politics, and socialism, and his own apartment became a meeting place for writers, artists, politicians, and policemen. The *Commercial Advertiser*'s circulation did not break records, but it climbed some, and the work of remaking its "good old grandmother" image was exhilarating.[23]

Steffens did not go out into the streets as much as he used to, but he maintained an active interest in reporting. In 1898, for example, he wrote a series of articles about the activities of Theodore Roosevelt. He had met Roosevelt three years before in 1895 when Roosevelt came to New York City to head the bipartisan Board of Police Commissioners and Steffens was in the thick of the Lexow police investigation. Steffens's autobiographical account of that time places both men in familiar roles: Roosevelt is the reckless innocent, charging about the city with colorful abandon; Steffens (with Jacob Riis) is his wise, restraining mentor who must show him where his new office is and tell him whom he should see first.

The memory bears little relation to the more complicated truth. The "Roosevelt Stories," as the 1898 articles were called, were somewhat more restrained.[24] Still, it was obvious that Steffens was interested in booming Roosevelt as a political personality, and his reports of Roosevelt's activities and opinions were creative, if they were also respectful. By that time Roosevelt had gone from President of the Police Board to Assistant Secretary of the Navy and from there, with the outbreak of the Spanish-American War in the spring of 1898, to Colonel of the Rough Riders. Now the war was over, and he was seeking the Republican nomination for the Governorship of New York. Steffens's stories promoted him as frank in private, cautious in public, brave in battle, and warm in the company of children.

Roosevelt would, in time, get his Governorship, then the Vice Presidency and finally, in 1901, the Presidency of the United States. Steffens kept up with him, continued to write about him, and engaged him in a dialogue of growing intimacy concerning public policy. Like him or not, Roosevelt was a personality no one could ignore for the next twenty years. Steffens's attitude toward him would shift during that time from enthusiasm to disgust to quiet condescension.

More interesting than the "Roosevelt Stories" were the articles Steffens wrote about himself. From his student years onward a small but important part of his imagination had been given over to autobiography. Up to now, however, he confined this sort of thinking to his correspondence. Then, in 1898 and 1899 it enjoyed a brief and more formal flowering. At the ripe age of thirty-two Steffens thought he had come some distance in life and wanted to write about it. He was a busy man now, as busy as he once told Fred Willis he wanted to be. Somehow, perhaps, that prompted him to remember his past in idyllic terms. In September 1898, he published "Heidelberg in Summer," a fond remembrance of university life with sketches of his old teachers, rowing on the river, and leisurely "second breakfasts" among friends. It was the first of seven articles in which he nostalgically recalled his past to life.[25] Some dealt with his boyhood, but most concerned his time in German universities; none of them relived any of the frustrations or anxieties which once had paralleled his real happiness there.

These sketches were extremely well done. Steffens's pen portraits of the people he knew are economical and acute, and his use of dialogue gave a sense of living interest to this news of yesterday. One must return to them in a later analysis of Steffens's much larger *Autobiography*, but it is worth noting here that the easy ambience of these early sketches is far different from the highly schematized version he would construct in the larger work.

One of these autobiographical pieces, shorter than

the rest and merely humorous in its intent is, perhaps,
a kind of personal estimation of his life to date. He
called it "An Unhappy Fishball" and represented himself
as chronically ambitious and unhappy. As a boy he lived in
a warm California valley but longed for snow to play in.
Then he loved a girl and was unhappy until she married
him. Next he wanted position and money and was vexed
until he had a better job and higher income. Now he de-
sires freedom and chafes at the restrictions of his job.
Last Sunday, he wrote, he wanted a fishball and searched
in vain for a restaurant that had one. "He wanted that
fishball," Steffens said of himself. "He didn't get it, and
he was never so unhappy as he was that evening."

He was joking, but there was a truth in what he wrote.
Steffens was not happy with his work. Neither were some
members of his own staff, if one is to believe the sketch
that Hutchins Hapgood wrote of him—called "An Interesting Failure"—in *Types from City Streets* (1910). Hapgood thought Steffens was too ambitious for big stories
and was losing his common touch. Steffens's editorship
would last two and a half more years and then he would
move again. When, in the spring of 1901, he told Henry
J. Wright, editor of the *Commercial Advertiser*, that *Mc-
Clure's Magazine* had invited him to become its Managing
Editor, Wright said he was sorry to lose him. "But,"
noted Steffens, "he did not resist." [26]

3

••••••••••••••••••••••••••••••••••••

Muckraker

The decade that began with Steffens's move to *McClure's Magazine* was a period of considerable growth for him personally and professionally. Latent talents flowered and he became famous. In the previous decade he had published skillful vignettes of city life which were buried in the back pages of newspapers or obscure magazines. But in the next ten years Steffens published long, well-considered articles in national monthlies and saw them collected in three successive books. *The Shame of the Cities* (1904) was followed by *The Struggle for Self-Government* (1906) and *Upbuilders* (1909). A playwright, George Broadhurst, even dramatized his revelations on the stages of New York and Philadelphia.[1] Steffens himself was in demand as a performer and began a successful second career as a public speaker. He had the pleasure of hearing people talk about him as he traveled from one engagement to the next, and a cigar manufacturer even asked to put his name and picture on a new brand of cigars. More seriously, President Theodore Roosevelt wrote him letters, sent him invitations to lunch, and frequently gave him a hearing, if not always his complete confidence.

His own self-confidence grew in these years, and he began to follow impulses to independence. Shortly after the turn of the century, for example, he started signing his work Lincoln Steffens, instead of Joseph or J. Lincoln Steffens, his father's name. He was to work on salary—a hundred dollars a week—for S. S. McClure, but after five years he joined the 1906 "palace revolt" at *McClure's* and withdrew, along with John S. Phillips, Ida M. Tarbell, Ray Stannard Baker and other staff members to buy and write for the *American Magazine*. Then, two years later, angry with the way his colleagues handled his copy, Steffens sold his *American* interests and became a free-lance writer with only occasional fixed responsibilities to the magazines for which he wrote. By that time, 1908, his name was well-known wherever it appeared.

It was well-known, and it was synonymous with "muckraking." And, no matter how interesting or worth recovering Steffens's 1890's newspaper writing is, he is remembered now less as a newspaper reporter and more as a muckraker. To be sure, the magazine articles which made up *Shame of the Cities* and the other books rested on his new sensitivity to human interest. But Steffens's muckraking pieces were more purposive than descriptive, and he composed them more with the reformer's sense of argument than the feature writer's more neutral aim of evoking a slice of life. Muckraking was more than mere argument, however, and there were many more muckrakers than Lincoln Steffens. What was muckraking, and how did Steffens come to join this movement in journalism?

Essentially, muckraking was a drive among journalists to ferret out and expose corrupt practices in business and government. The names of the magazines are largely forgotten now, but for a time between 1901 and about 1914 *McClure's, Collier's, Cosmopolitan, Everybody's, Hampton's* and *American* built impressive circulations with assaults on big city politicos, patent medicines, industrial monopolies, and "white slavery." None of these magazines began as muckrakers. In the 1890's they were mostly family monthlies that catered to a middle class interest in uncontroversial news of progress and personalities, on one hand, and sentimental romance on the other.

Then, suddenly, around the turn of the century, magazines which had been bland and reassuring adopted a reform posture and started spreading news that all was not well in America. This shift, impressive not just for its quickness but for the range of magazines which took up the new pose, occurred for a variety of reasons. The Spanish-American War of 1898 quickened popular interest in the conduct and failures of public policy, while the trend toward business monopoly and its dramatic acceleration after 1898 spread fear that the men who controlled America's economic institutions had abandoned old ideals of democracy and open competition. People who had never given much thought to public questions wondered what else was wrong with America. The muckrakers gave them the answers.

Muckraking was also exciting as literature. Villainous robber barons, pathetic victims, and heroic reformers were fascinating characters whose dress and dialogue often relieved the serious factual exposition of a typical muckraking article. In that sense, magazine editors held fast to a formula which had served them well in the previous decade: no matter what the subject, a magazine piece must be interesting, enthralling if possible. No periodical's circulation sky-rocketed in the muckraking era, but each one made steady gains.

Muckraking flourished from about 1901 to 1914. It began to wane when readers became sated with the exposure style and when offended advertisers threatened to withdraw support. Then too, President Theodore Roosevelt, who had encouraged the first exposures and had lent his favorite writers—Steffens among them—a certain legitimacy with invitations to the White House, began to draw back. In 1906 Roosevelt attacked all the muckrakers in a sweeping indictment which gave them their unofficial but lasting name. They were like "the man with the muckrake" in John Bunyan's *Pilgrim's Progress,* he said, too busy scraping the filth at his feet to notice the bigger blue sky above. Roosevelt was a popular president, and the same prestige that had for a time made a magazine like *McClure's* read like an unofficial organ of Roosevelt's "Square Deal" began thereafter to strip muckraking of its attraction.[2]

Steffens became disillusioned with muckraking before the movement lost its general vogue, but while he was part of it the sense of creating and belonging to something larger than himself was exhilarating and contributed to his growing self-confidence. He was gregarious and liked the long, sometimes disputacious staff lunches at New York's Holland House with his fellow muckrakers Ida M. Tarbell, Ray Stannard Baker and others.

Self-confidence showed in his writing, too. Each of his major works requires detailed, individual analysis, but some general points can be made here. For one thing, each successive collection of articles from *Shame of the Cities* through *Struggle for Self-Government* and *Upbuilders* revealed an increase in militancy and personal engagement. The early essays on St. Louis and Minneapolis in *Shame of the Cities* are largely free of sweeping generalizations about all political society, but the book's later essays, though they also concern specific cities, are more broadly interpretive. Steffens's next two books are filled with a new self-assurance and, often, cocky moral pronouncement.

Yet sometimes the tone of street-wise authority masked a layer of uncertainty. He was not as naive during these years as the *Autobiography* makes him out, but his muckraking was nonetheless often a mixture of penetrating realism, unschooled idealism, and embarrassing sentimentalism. He was realistic, for example, in pointing out the difference between the constitutional description of government and public office, on one hand, and the actual, less visible operation of government on the other. His insistence that official rhetoric and private behavior were not the same thing was a simple but important concept.

Then, in other parts of his writing, Steffens seemed to forget this lesson himself and slip into naive, uncritical expectations. He imagined that "the people," abused by corrupt governments, existed apart from economic, religious, and geographical interest groups, and he was often puzzled by their disinclination to rise as a body to throw off their oppressors once they were taught who the oppressors were. He seemed in such moods to think that reform was only a matter of substituting patriotic office-holders for special interest men and "general legislation" for laws benefitting railroad magnates, steel monopolists and other businessmen. Furthermore, though Steffens finally saw that President Theodore Roosevelt was as much politician as statesman, he was beguiled too long with the notion that Roosevelt was a powerful but pure reformer who sought only the mandate of "the people." Even after he began to see Roosevelt clearly, he still was capable of writing articles which imagined that reform would come at the hands of humble, even meek men whom he described variously as gentle, feline or "sweet-faced."

Steffens would later organize his autobiography around his passage from ignorance to understanding. But evidence from the muckraking pieces themselves suggests that such a view was no mere hindsight. For all his strident posturing, Steffens seemed to know he did not understand everything yet. His tales of city politics were often cast in polarities, with reformers and bosses representing ignorance and knowledge respectively. Steffens seemed to admire the bosses—men like Cincinnati's George Cox, for example—because, despite their uncouth brutality, they possessed what he wanted: knowledge. They had knowledge of their cities but also of human nature itself. He could like the reformers, too, but only at the point when, as citizens, they cast off their innocence and began to acquire a tough-mindedness equal to that of their corrupt adversaries. Otherwise he had no use for them.

When S. S. McClure hired him as *McClure's* new

Managing Editor, however, Steffens seemed as knowledgeable a man for the job as he could get. The magazine's
editorial staff liked the literary tone he had given the
Commercial Advertiser but they liked his background in
political and economic reporting as well. *McClure's* was
in the midst of an important change in the spring of
1901, a transition, still only half-conscious in the minds of
McClure and his associate, John S. Phillips, to muckraking
and reform. The Spanish-American War had moved *Mc-
Clure's* to commit itself on public questions for the first
time since its founding in 1893. By the time Steffens arrived at *McClure's* in September 1901, the magazine was
firmly settled into its new public-interest editorial stance.
Ida M. Tarbell was already at work writing her exposure
of the Standard Oil Company and Ray Stannard Baker
was readying a critical and dramatic dissection of labor
relations. Phillips's eagerness to have Steffens, a newspaperman, join the staff was confirmation of his and Mc-
Clure's desire to put more "news" into their magazine.[3]

The Shame of the Cities (1904)

But if Steffens came to his desk with the title of
Managing Editor, he did not last long either as a desk
man or as an editor. For in December S. S. McClure
himself returned to New York from an editorial foraging
expedition and told him to get out. "You can't learn to
edit a magazine here in this office," he said, and when
Steffens asked where he could learn, McClure made a
wide circle with his hand and replied: "Anywhere else.
Get out of here, travel, go—somewhere. Go out in the advertising department. Ask them where they have transportation credit. Buy a railroad ticket, get on a train, and
there, where it lands you, there you will learn to edit a
magazine." [4] McClure's command was in keeping with his
own belief in travel and personal contact, and because

Steffens did not like office work anyway, he adopted Mc-
Clure's method. Much of the executive work that should
have been done by Steffens had already been taken over
by another young man, Albert C. Boyden, a recent Harvard graduate and Phillips's son-in-law, who had been in
the office a few months before Steffens came. Over the
next several months, as Steffens wrote more and edited
less, Boyden emerged as Phillips's chief lieutenant in New
York.

McClure's had an advertising bill against the Lacka-
wanna Railroad, and in May 1902, Steffens rode to Chicago with a list of writers and public figures to interview,
suggested by Boyden, who also told him to stop and see
his brother, a Chicago attorney. After attending to a few
minor editorial matters and following up his list without
success, Steffens visited Boyden's brother and learned of
the fight Joseph W. Folk, prosecuting attorney for St.
Louis, was waging against bribery and corruption in that
municipal government. McClure had apparently suggested
that city and state governments might be ripe for dramatic treatment, and the prospect of an article on St.
Louis rekindled Steffens's own interest in urban government. He visited Folk in St. Louis and then wrote back to
New York that if the magazine took up state governments,
the magazine should ask William Allen White, the emerging
reform journalist from Kansas, to do it, but if *McClure's*
was to have a series on cities, he wanted to handle it himself. "If I should be trusted with the work," he said, "I
think I could make my name." [5]

Steffens interviewed Folk and learned that he had
been boosted to his post as district attorney by "Boss" Ed
Butler as an outsider in an effort to settle a quarrel among
several machine candidates for the job. Now he was carrying out his duty in a way Butler had not expected,
trying to break the power of St. Louis's Democratic machine. Folk wanted the magazine's assistance in publiciz-
ing his campaign. Since Steffens's position was still that of

an editor in search of ideas, he agreed, but hired Claude
H. Wetmore, a local reporter, to write an article about
St. Louis and send it to New York for editing. When
Steffens read Wetmore's article, he was disappointed that
the reporter had played down Ed Butler's personal role
in corruption, so he added a few details about him on his
own, cosigning the article when Wetmore protested that
he could not continue to work in the city if Steffens's
insertions appeared as his. Steffens first called the piece
"St. Louis Upside Down"—a sober title—but after some
thought changed it to "Tweed Days in St. Louis," to re-
flect his own growing consciousness that the business-political axis Folk had discovered in his city was not unique
—that "Boss" Ed Butler had his counterpart in the legendary "Boss" William Marcy Tweed of New York and in
scores of bosses everywhere.

At first, McClure envisioned the series of articles
which became *Shame of the Cities* as an international
study to include Birmingham, England and Naples, Italy,
but Steffens finally limited it to six American cities: St.
Louis (two articles), Minneapolis, Pittsburgh, Philadelphia, Chicago and New York. He researched and wrote
the rest of the articles himself and they appeared irregularly in *McClure's* between October 1902 and November
1903. The following year the McClure publishing house
issued them as a book.

Considering its reputation as an original and influential book, it may be wise to begin an evaluation of *Shame
of the Cities* by making clear what it was not. For one
thing, it was not a series of stunning new facts pulled
out of reluctant sources and never revealed before. Steffens, of course, never claimed that it was, and, in fact,
one of his stated reasons for writing was to publicize
not only the things people did not know about corruption
in their cities but also the *fact* that they knew things and
allowed them to continue anyway. This complacent knowledge was itself the "shame" of Minneapolis or any other

city. Much of Steffens's information came from open court
testimony and public reports of local citizens' reform
groups, while considerably less of his reporting came from
personal contacts with the bribers and boodlers themselves. And, though he and the other muckrakers became
famous for naming names and fixing places in articles
that were supposed to have been as thorough as grand
jury indictments, Steffens's names and places came from
public documents with established legal pedigrees. Not in-
frequently when he did have private information, he omit-
ted the principals' names with conspicuous blank spaces
or replaced them with general terms like "Mr. Council-
man."

If the result often made Steffens a mere summarizer
of known graft prosecutions, his very summarizing became
a revelation in the broader sense that readers in one city
may have realized for the first time that corruption was
everywhere. The articles had a powerful cumulative effect,
and Steffens could ask, given so many incidents of corruption, whether vice and bribery were not really a problem of the total American culture. The asking of such a
question (discussed further below) revealed at least a
new category of thinking about old, known problems.

Further, *The Shame of the Cities* was not a syste-
matic treatise on urban government cast in a well-artic-
ulated theoretical framework. Above all it was a popular
magazine series, largely descriptive and often dramatic
with the clashing of personalities in brilliantly highlighted
bits of dialogue. Later, when Steffens relived the writing
of the articles in his autobiography, he stressed his development of a "theory of graft" which soon bulked so
large that McClure and the rest of the staff began to resist
it. Yet a reading of the pieces themselves reveals that
Steffens hinted at and implied more about corruption as
a function of American culture than he fully argued.

Nonetheless, whatever they lacked in careful exposition, Steffens's ideas were there, and three of them may

be singled out as themes in *The Shame of the Cities*. The first, that businessmen's private needs always took precedence over the public good, was prefigured in a bitter essay Steffens published in October 1901, many months before he first visited Joseph Folk in St. Louis but after a varied observation of the New York political scene. In "Great Types of Modern Business—Politics" he attacked the notion that reform could best be achieved by electing businessmen to office since business was the very corruptor of social and political life in the first place. "Politics is a business," he said.

That's what's the matter with it! That's what is the matter with everything—art, literature, religion, journalism, law, medicine—they're all business and all—as you see them. Make politics a sport, as they do in England, or a profession, as they do in Germany, and we'll have—well, something else than we have now, if we want it, which is another question. But don't try to reform politics with the banker, the lawyer and the drygoods merchant, for these are businessmen. . . .[6]

When Steffens wrote a preface to bring the articles together as *The Shame of the Cities* in 1904, he simply inserted this paragraph and others from the earlier essay and then went on to elaborate the point. Businessmen were guilty on two counts: once because the biggest among them offered bribes to politicians in order to secure lucrative franchises and city contract business, and again because the smaller "average" businessmen were careless and neglectful of government—the good of the community—as they followed the narrow line of private money-making. The charge against the big men was the easiest to objectify in the articles themselves, so Steffens filled his accounts with images of well-dressed men negotiating traction deals and placing fat packets of cash in safe deposit boxes when the time for political payoffs drew near. The parallel charge concerning the average businessman's unthinking neglect was harder to portray, but

Steffens could at least imagine him as a type and put
words into his mouth:

When his neglect has permitted bad government to go so far
that he can be stirred to action, he is unhappy, and he looks
around for a cure that shall be quick, so that he may hurry
back to the shop. Naturally, too, when he talks politics, he
talks shop. His patent remedy is quack; it is business.

"Give us a businessman," he says, ("like me," he
means). "Let him introduce business methods into politics
and govenment; then I shall be left alone to attend to my
business." [7]

Related to the problem presented by businessmen was
a second theme: that the chief blame for corruption in
government rested not with the grafters and boodlers
but with their victims, "the people," for they were the
ones who knew it was happening and did not rise to stop
it. Steffens claimed this idea came to him gradually as he
travelled from one city to the next, but later he said in
his autobiography that he first saw the principle when he
went to the race track as a boy and learned from the
jockeys how horse races were fixed so that the favorite
who, by all the visible standards of judgment—pedigree,
jockey, previous record—ought to win was held back to
lose. But the people in the stands ("suckers" Steffens
learned to call them, including one day his father) did
not want to hear about the fix and bet money on horses
whose chances they judged by the usual standards. It was
they, the boy decided, who made the fix possible. And
it was millions more of them in American society who
made municipal corruption possible. "The people are not
innocent," he wrote after the last article was published.
"That is the only 'news' in all the journalism of these
articles. . . ." [8]

Whatever its origin, the idea was rooted in Steffens's
assumption that men could be moved by one of two con-

flicting interests, the public and the private, and his assumption, too, that citizens were aware of the difference
and were therefore responsible for the choice they made
one way or the other. They could vote for the boodlers
or they could vote for "St. Louis," but they had no right
to expect anything more than what they chose. Steffens's
categories tended to be starkly drawn and allowed for little qualification. Citizens confronted with this simple choice
were generally just "the people," or "the Pittsburghers."
In Minneapolis they were stereotyped to fit the region
as "Miles, Hans and Ole," but Steffens did not recognize
differentiation among them according to where they lived,
how much they earned, or where they went to church.
One gets the impression, reading the essays today, that
Steffens did not know his cities as well as his reputation
for thoroughness suggested.

The people seldom chose the public interest because
they were gullible and easily taken in by politics organized around parties. No one questioned the need for
party organization and no one asked whether or not there
was another choice beyond Republicans and Democrats
even when it was clear that neither party represented
anything above the interests of the few. Steffens hoped to
shame urban citizens into rising against parties and reach-
ing consciousness as an independent third force which
would have only the public good in mind when it went
to the polls.

At times Steffens seemed to reject political organization altogether, and his argument was then reminiscent
of the fears manifested by George Washington, James
Madison, and others among the founding fathers who
cautioned against the rise of political parties on the
grounds that parties embodied only factional interests and
would create permanent and threatening divisiveness. But
elsewhere he argued more realistically that good government was possible if the people could find and follow
leaders who had the community in mind and would use a

political methodology borrowed from the very politicians they wanted to beat. America was a country in which demand called forth supply, he argued, and if bosses and their machines thrived on supplying what a few private interests demanded, the people need only create a demand for government in the public interest and give their votes to new political organizations that would supply it.

How could this be done? Steffens insisted that *The Shame of the Cities* was not a manual of reform, but he did demonstrate the possibilities for success or failure by reviewing the cases of St. Louis, in all its "shamelessness," and Chicago, "Half Free and Fighting On." Steffens wrote two articles on St. Louis and together they are a detailed chronicle of bribery and election fraud well-known, he claimed, to the people of St. Louis and presided over by Colonel Ed Butler, boss of the city's Democratic machine. At the beginning of "Tweed Days in St. Louis" Joseph W. Folk emerges unexpectedly as a lone fighter against Butler's machine, and the article shows him single-handedly uncovering an empire of corruption. The second article, "The Shamelessness of St. Louis," takes the story through Folk's prosecutions to the trial of Butler himself in the fall of 1902. Butler was on his way to conviction, and the forthcoming November elections offered the opportunity for the people to rise. But then nothing happened. The machine made up its ticket as usual and when election day came citizens who might have opposed the machine as an independent force had not even bothered to register. "Butler, the papers said, had great furniture vans going about with men who were said to be repeaters, and yet the registration was the lowest in many years." At the end of the article, but in the middle of his term, Folk is as alone as when he began. "The convicts sitting in the municipal assembly, the convicts appealing to the higher courts, the rich man abroad, the bankers down town— all are waiting for something," wrote Steffens. "What are they waiting for?" The answer, a warning, he put in the mouth of a Butler henchman: "I am waiting for Joe Folk's term to expire. Then I am going home to run for Governor of Missouri and vindication." [9]

But Chicago was a different story. For years "everybody was for himself, and no one for Chicago" until in 1895 civic-minded men formed the Municipal Voters' League—"the Nine," as they came to be called—headed by George E. Cole. Cole's virtue was that he was a businessman who had sense enough to know that he needed a *political* solution to Chicago's problems. Suggestions that there be more newspaper exposures and more graft prosecutions were set aside in favor of direct political intervention in the municipal elections of 1895. First the Nine published the records of corrupt Aldermen running for re-election and then, by threatening to publish more sensitive information, they blackmailed many of them into retirement. Next, Cole's group worked at the ward level to influence the make-up of party tickets. They did not insist upon total honesty, just more honesty—"a likely rascal to beat the rascal that was in and known"—among the candidates the Nine supported. They offered decisive League support to the minority party's candidate in exchange for a say in who the candidate would be. Steffens summed up their accomplishments: "I should say that the basic unstated principle of this reform movement, struck out early in the practice of the Nine, was to let the politicians rule, but through better and better men whom the Nine forced upon them with public opinion." [10] What made it all work, of course, was the crystallization of that public opinion. Steffens did not go into why the "Chicagoans" rose to the occasion when the "St. Louisans" could not; it was enough for him to know that they did.

The question was, of course, which case was typical, St. Louis or Chicago? Steffens hoped it was Chicago but seemed to suspect that it was St. Louis, and his suspicion was related to the third theme in *Shame of the Cities*:

that corruption was the necessary product of American culture. The repeated incidence of corruption from one city to the next was enough to suggest a cultural interpretation. "Evidently," he once told S. S. McClure, "you could shoot me out of a gun fired at random and, wherever I lighted, there would be a story, the same way." [11] But did the scope of it mean it was peculiarly American? A standard explanation assured that it was not, that corruption was carried like a disease to America with the current waves of foreign immigrants; wherever they went it would flourish. But Steffens visited Philadelphia, "the most American of our greater cities" with 47 per cent of its population native born of native parents, and found it "corrupt and contented," the worst-governed city in the country. Nor, as others suggested, was bad government a function of youth, for he found it in the oldest cities as well as the newest.

Still the closest Steffens came to a theory of his own, apart from noting the neglect of the people and the powerful private drives unleashed by the commercial spirit, was a vague suggestion in the Philadelphia article that cities must pass through "typical stages of corruption," from a period of "miscellaneous loot with a boss for chief thief" at one end to "absolutism" at the other. New York in the 1860s under Tweed was an example of the first stage, and St. Louis was at present just emerging from that stage. Evolution through the middle stages was not spelled out, but Philadelphia represented something dangerously close to the last stage. This was so not just because Philadelphians were largely disenfranchised ("The honest citizens of Philadelphia have no more rights at the polls than the negroes down South"), but because it was run by a city Republican machine which was controlled by a state Republican machine which was itself tied to the national Republican organization. "This is the ideal of party organization," he wrote, "and, possibly, is the end toward which our democratic republic is tending. If it is, the end is absolutism. Nothing but a revolution could overthrow this oligarchy, and there is its danger." [12]

On the whole, however, Steffens's theories, even when connected to such stark warnings, were probably of more interest to himself than they were to his readers. What attracted them more was the impression he gave of the scope of corrupt politics and, beyond that, his extraordinary skill at sheer characterization, a literary rather than a scientific approach. What distinguished Steffens from other journalists was his keen sense of how things *looked*: a careful eye for appearances and the symbolic value thrown up by objective data. In his autobiography, for example, he relates the story of his arrival in Pittsburgh on a night in 1903 to muckrake the town for *McClure's*. He decided to take a walk around the streets before retiring, and his rambles finally brought him to a hill overlooking the huge, fire-belching furnaces of the steel mills. The might and mystery of what he saw impressed Steffens powerfully as the symbol of the city, and he wrote back to New York for an artist—not merely an illustrator, he recalled—to capture it on canvas for *McClure's*. Jules Guerin's painting "Pittsburgh as Hell with the Lid Off" appeared with Steffens's own "Pittsburgh: A City Ashamed" in May 1903.[13] In other cities he searched for unusual portraits of the bosses whose sordid tales he spread on the magazine's pages, or he might look for facsimiles of the handwritten "contract" which governed the dealings of one boss with another. In St. Louis he found photographs of expensive, half-finished public buildings already falling to ruin as symbols of the city's moral and material rot. Unfortunately, few of these pictures were reprinted in *The Shame of the Cities* when it was issued as a book.

But often prose was enough. Language—the careful choice of words—could do as much as anything to call the reader's attention to the articles' contents. McClure said he wanted words like "shame" and phrases like "enemies of the republic" scattered throughout the muckrake pieces because they shocked people and heightened the effect of bad news appearing month by month in the magazine, so Steffens wrote "The Shame of Minneapolis," "The Shamelessness of St. Louis," and "Pittsburgh: A City Ashamed."

Yet language was only the beginning. The real attraction of Steffens's work was his skill at weaving tales of corruption around personalities. Whatever his theories, no impersonal forces of economics or demography really shaped Steffens's cities; they were in the grip of bosses and reformers with sharply defined personal histories and characters. Almost every city had a boss like St. Louis's Ed Butler or Minneapolis's "Doc" Ames, and when there were two bosses in one city, they worked as one. Thus Steffens described Chris Magee and William Flinn of Pittsburgh as two parts of a split personality: "Magee wanted power, Flinn wanted wealth. Each got both these things; but Magee spent his wealth for more power, and Flinn spent his power for more wealth. Magee was the sower, Flinn the reaper. In dealing with men they came to be necessary to each other, these two. Magee attracted followers, Flinn employed them. The men Magee won, Flinn compelled to obey, and those he lost Magee won back." [14] And the bosses were brazen, cocky men, all seeming to mouth Boss William Marcy Tweed's earlier famous taunt, "What are you going to do about it?" When they talked to Steffens they seemed willing to spill all with a smiling assurance that no one could touch them. Steffens made as much of this as he could because he, too, wanted to taunt his readers, to repeat and amplify the insult with the intention of goading them into action.

Steffens described the reformers, too, so that his articles emphasized characteristics which tended to "type" them. They all seemed to resemble St. Louis's Joseph W. Folk, "a thin-lipped, firm-mouthed, dark little man, who never raises his voice." Quiet-spoken, ordinary citizens—perhaps the way Steffens imagined his own readers—the reformers were at first reluctant to leave private life and start fights with the bosses, but once involved, they fought tenaciously, uncompromisingly in ways that must command the respect of the bosses themselves. If a bank president refuses to open a safe deposit box to reveal a suspected bundle of bribery cash and pleads in fearful, "almost inaudible tones" for time to consult legal advice, Folk says: "We will wait ten minutes." If the prosecuting attorney for Minneapolis is too frightened to attack "Doc" Ames, then Hovey Clarke, foreman of the grand jury says simply: "You are excused." There is a scene. " 'Do you think, Mr. Clarke,' he cried, 'that you can run the grand jury and my office, too?' 'Yes,' said Clarke, 'I will run your office if I want to; and I want to. You're excused.' " [15]

Writing in terms of personalities had been standard policy at *McClure's* for a decade, well before the magazine's muckrake phase, but it was especially useful in Steffens's work. Another tested device was to write part or all of an article as the story of the reporter's own visit to the people involved. Steffens was just learning to use this device to give a sense of the urgent present to articles which otherwise often dealt with the history of one or another city's corruption. He reported conversations with citizens about local politics and gave his readers tours of cities' decaying streets in an effort to bring home the very present physical consequences of bad government.

The Shame of the Cities made Steffens famous for his detailed exposition of corruption in high places. Yet he also knew when to avoid masses of detail in favor of a more careful and sparse selection of symbolic events—things which would stay in a reader's mind the longer because they stood alone and uncluttered on the page. Steffens measured the distance which "Doc" Ames had traveled toward moral degeneracy, for example, by offer-

ing two sketches of the Minneapolis boss: in one Ames is
a young doctor helping the poor without charge ("Richer
men than you will pay your bill") ; in the other an older
Ames has neglected his family, left his wife for another
woman, and now sits in a carriage outside the wife's
funeral, "with his feet up and a cigar in his mouth, till
the funeral moved; then he circled around, crossing it
and meeting it, and making altogether a scene which
might well close any man's career." [16]

Both Steffens's critique of urban America and the
manner in which he expressed it had one thing in common: they were both models of a new kind of journalism
aimed at specific social change. "I wanted to move and to
convince," he said when the last article was published.[17]
Such a concept of journalism was not new in itself, of
course, for others had understood the power of the press
before him. Joseph Pulitzer's New York *World* had been
using sensationalism as a tool for social awareness and
change since the 1880s, and some of Steffens's own newspaper work during the 1890s had leaned in that direction. But these had been local efforts aimed at local problems. *The Shame of the Cities* united substance with style
in an attempt to create a national reform consciousness,
and the popularity of his work was some measure of his
success.

The Shame of the Cities did not sell much over 3000
copies in book form, but that plus the articles' large circulation in *McClure's*—370,000 for 1903—gave Steffens his
first national readership. "It is being reviewed everywhere," Steffens told his father early in April 1904, two
weeks after the book appeared, "and, together with the
last article, is making quite a stir. Maybe I'll beat some
of the novels." [18] The last sentence could have had dou-
ble meaning. He had once hoped to write novels and
follow a traditional literary career, and he still published
stories in magazines. But now it was journalism, with
its cross between reportage and imagination, that drew

him on. Journalism, originally the preparation for a career, was now career enough, satisfying Steffens's scientific need to document and order social reality, while at the same time giving an outlet for his artistic sense of scene and character.

The Struggle for Self-Government (1906)

No sooner had Steffens seen his first book through the press than he began work on his next. The April 1904 issue of *McClure's* carried "Folk's Fight for Missouri," the first article in a new series on corruption in the states which, together with six more articles, would appear as *The Struggle for Self-Government* in 1906. He traveled and worked on the new series through the next year. Following the Missouri article in April, the magazine published "Chicago's Appeal to Illinois" in April 1904; "Wisconsin: Representative Government Restored," in October; "Rhode Island: A Corrupted People" in February 1905; "New Jersey: A Traitor State" (in two parts) in April and May; and "Ohio: A Tale of Two Cities" in July. The Ohio piece, last to appear, had originally been planned as the first article, but much of it was an attack on Marcus A. Hanna, Ohio's senior United States Senator and boss of its Republican machine, and when Hanna sickened and died a month before scheduled publication, McClure put it off more than a year.[19]

The Struggle for Self-Government was in many ways the logical follow-up to *The Shame of the Cities*. Steffens had discovered that whenever corrupt businessmen or politicians were beaten in one or another city, they could always retreat to the state capital. State governments often had power to legislate for certain strictly municipal functions, like transportation and utility franchises, so what boodlers could not get from reformed city councils they could get from corrupt state legislatures. Reformers, like

Joseph Folk of St. Louis, could only follow them to the capital for a final showdown. Steffens went too, in a sense, describing the boodlers' retreat and the reformers' pursuit in *The Struggle for Self-Government*.

Discovering the connection between city and state government seemed to make Steffens more eager to draw lengthy, explicit generalizations about politics. Passages in some articles are frankly didactic. *"Political corruption, then,"* begins one italicized, textbookish proposition in the Illinois article, *"is a force by which a representative democracy is transformed into an oligarchy representative of special interests, and the medium of the revolution is the party."* [20] His brilliant evocation of place and personality was still an integral element of his writing—many scenes and dialogues were more compelling than in *Shame of the Cities*—but it was also obvious that Steffens wanted more room than before for strictly theoretical exposition.

As he moved from the city to the state, Steffens found that his politicos' behavior did not change. Since city and state politicians were merely parts of one system, there was no reason to expect a change. What he did discover were new, broader, more intense demonstrations of the patterns already familiar to readers of *Shame of the Cities*: the precedence of business over public interest, the ignorant guilt of the people, and the cultural root of political corruption.

As Steffens reported it in *Shame of the Cities*, the primacy of business interests was a threat of serious but local proportions. The language he used to criticize businessmen was most often the language of contempt. In *Struggle for Self-Government*, however, he saw business interests as a fundamental, national challenge to the very concept of popular government. Americans, imagining, perhaps, official constitutions and charters, liked to think they had representative government. Steffens pointed out that the phrase "representative government" meant nothing and merely begged a question. All governments, he

said, were representative; the question was *whom* did
American city, state and national governments represent,
and the answer was corrupt business. New Jersey's government represented the Pennsylvania Railroad, Rhode Island's, through its powerful Senator Nelson W. Aldrich,
represented "Sugar," "Standard Oil," and "Wall Street."
In Missouri, government was for a time in the hands of
the baking powder industry. Rival companies fought the
notorious "alum war" over whether alum leavening was
poisonous. Mindful only of profits, company officials
bribed state legislators and corrupted the integrity of scientists as though the possibility of alum poisoning was
no issue at all. Constitutions and charters notwithstand-
ing, America's real form of government seemed to be
corruption itself. "Our political corruption is a system,"
Steffens wrote, "a regularly established custom of the
country, by which our political leaders are hired, by
bribery, by the license to loot, and by quiet moral support,
to conduct the government of city, State and Nation, not
for the common good, but for the special interests of
private business." [21]

In the face of such an all-pervasive system, were the
people of the states as guilty through sheer complacence
as the citizens of the cities had been? Initially, Steffens
answered yes, reaffirming the second theme of *The Shame
of the Cities*. He introduced *Struggle for Self-Government* with a savagely ironic dedication "To His Majesty,
Nicholas the Second, By the Grace of God, Emperor and
Autocrat of all the Russias, Czar of Poland, Grand Duke
of Finland, etc., etc." Czarist Russia had long stood in
the American imagination as the archetype of tyrannical
government. But in the spring of 1906, when Steffens's
book appeared, Russia was still rocking in the wake of the
Revolution of 1905. American newspapers had carried reports of uprisings and repression for a year. The revolution failed but Czar Nicholas promised to convene a rep-

resentative assembly, the Duma, which, however, he so circumscribed and restricted that it was without power.

Steffens's dedication chided the Czar for fearing representative government and learning nothing from the American example. The Americans had won a revolution, too, in 1776, but it hardly mattered because a second revolution, "nameless and slow," had now been under way for some time whereby business and businessmen were taking step-by-step control of the government. They began with the cities, moved next to the states, and now threatened the federal government itself. It happened in America because the people, whose own original revolution was being obliterated, just did not seem to care. Neither, Steffens advised the Czar, would the Russian people even if they won their first revolution. They cannot see that there is a difference between charter government and actual government, so they will not even notice that the second revolution is happening. Like Americans, they will prefer order to power anyway. The best which even the dissidents—the reformers—in America have been capable of is an occasional mild revolt against one or another business-government deal. The telling characteristic of such reform, however, is its irregularity. The people do not want continuing control of their government. The Czar could therefore grant a full, liberal constitution and still rule through easy manipulation of that very constitution. American cities and states have their constitutions, but they have their "Czars" and "Grand Dukes," too.

Steffens's tone was bitter and his "dedication" adopted the pose of giving up on the American people. Still, he seems to have only half believed that the time had come to throw up his hands. For when he prepared the original *McClure's* articles for book publication, he footnoted the last line of each one with the good news that in each of the six states except Rhode Island—which

had a "corrupted people" and was beyond hope—popular reform movements were now under way. The elections of 1905 made Joseph Folk Governor of Missouri,
Charles S. Deneen Governor of Illinois, and Robert La-
Follette Governor of Wisconsin. In Ohio, the people of
Cincinnati threw out Boss George Cox, while Toledo
elected Steffens's friend Brand Whitlock mayor and Cleveland re-elected Mayor Tom Johnson. In the same year,
New Jersey launched "a promising movement for representative government" led by State Senator Everett
Colby. Whatever ambivalence Steffens felt toward "the
people," election week was at least exhilarating. He reviewed the results with Toledo's Brand Whitlock and
summed it all up: "In other words, we, the American
people, carried ourselves at last, and the beginning has
been made toward the restoration of representative democracy in all the land." [22]

Despite his initial harsh answer to the question of the
people's guilt, redemption sometimes seemed possible after all, though Steffens would often be unsure about the
means. Sometimes the electorate awakened for no dis-
cernible reason. Folk, he pointed out, alone among Democrats in a "Republican year," won in Missouri, and he
did so despite the fact that ticket-splitting was difficult in
Missouri. More and more, however, it seemed that a single
tough man with good intentions and a machine of his own
was the least requirement. In the 1905 elections, Robert
LaFollette demonstrated that with a vengeance. Steffens's
article about LaFollette's career in Wisconsin was a kind of
essay in political method, holding the same place in *Struggle for Self-Government* that "Chicago: Half Free and
Fighting On" did in *Shame of the Cities*. "The story of
the State of Wisconsin is the story of Governor LaFollette," Steffens wrote, particularly the story of his self-
conscious fashioning of a political machine oiled with the
promises, patronage and loyalty normally associated with

the corrupt business-political organization LaFollette had to beat. LaFollette's opponents, Steffens claimed, urged that he come to Wisconsin and muckrake the LaFollette "ring," with its demands of loyalty and the tight exclusivity of its membership. Steffens came, but by the time he left to write his article, having seen the Governor's general administration of justice and no special consideration for special interests, his report could be summarized in a single short sentence: "There is a machine, but it is LaFollette's." [23] And that made all the difference.

The same ambivalence on whether reform was possible that ran through *Shame of the Cities* pervaded *Struggle for Self-Government*. Steffens's first book began with cautious optimism but seemed to move on a zigzag course toward warning and doubt. The second book began with doubt (transformed into sarcasm in the dedication to Czar Nicholas), but attempted a return to optimism. The question of reform was still open, obviously, and for Steffens it would remain that way for a long time to come.

The optimism did not make sense considering that Steffens still seemed to think that corruption was culturally determined, inevitable. That point had been a third theme in *Shame of the Cities*, and, if anything, he argued it more elaborately in *Struggle for Self-Government*. The first book suggested that cities passed through definable stages of corruption from "miscellaneous looting" to absolutism, and Steffens hinted that in the case of Philadelphia, at least, the line of corruption went from the city to the state and from there to the national government. In his second book, these suggestions solidified into convictions. There was, indeed, an almost complete system of corruption in America. Drawing, perhaps, on the naturalism of his student years, he saw society as an integrated organism so shot through with disease that cures applied to single organs were unavailing:

Every time I attempted to trace to its sources the political corruption of a city ring, the stream of pollution branched off in the most unexpected directions and spread out in a network of veins and arteries so complex that hardly any part of the body politic seemed clear of it. It flowed out of the majority party into the minority; out of politics into vice and crime; out of business into politics, and back into business; from the boss down through the police to the prostitute, and up through the practice of law into the courts; and big throbbing arteries ran out through the country over the State to the Nation—and back. No wonder cities can't get municipal reform! [24]

The names of the participants—bosses, businessmen, governors—were now familiar, yet no one politician had ever envisioned the system whole or had consciously set about building it as such. Rather it emerged from social and historical forces larger than individual men. Specifically, business enterprise—the force of economics—was the cultural driving force. Businessmen corrupted politics not as an end in itself but as the means to the end of making money. No evil geniuses despoiled popular government out of sheer perversion. Even Mark Hanna, boss of Ohio and "king-maker" of national Republican politics, only corrupted governments in Ohio as a secondary effect of a more immediate goal: securing lucrative trolley car franchises for himself and his friends. Steffens found the same lack of intent when he interviewed William Zeigler, who had corrupted legislatures, governors, newspapers and scientists in Missouri's "alum war." Steffens explained to Zeigler how his business requirements had warped the very political society of Missouri. Then their conversation continued:

"I didn't want to do that," he said over and over again. "I simply did not see it so. I fought each fight as it came up."

"Yes," I said, "you business men say, as if you were wise, that you cross bridges when you come to them."

"I certainly did not mean to change the government." [25]

It was by no means certain yet, but Steffens was on the edge of deciding that men like Hanna and Zeigler were not guilty in the ordinary use of the word. In the strictly legal sense, they could be prosecuted for what they did, and a few did even go to jail. But in a larger sense, they were only responding to larger economic forces which made them less responsible for the result. They had a kind of crude honesty about them and, in any case, Steffens was coming to like them.

Steffens's ideas about corruption—its business backing, its victims and their guilt, and its roots in large historical forces—were elaborated from suggestions given first in *Shame of the Cities.* Those ideas and their fuller expression were what *Struggle for Self-Government* was explicitly about.

But Steffens was more than a straightforward political analyst. He was a journalist, with the best qualities that term implies, and he was also something of an artist. His desire to characterize reality as well as explain it meant that the style of his writing and the manner of his constructions would carry as much of his argument as explicit statements of it.

The language of irony—attaching alien characteristics to situations that do not warrant them—could be used to invest commonplace events with special meaning. Steffens described deals between business moguls and politicians as so widespread, for example, that he sometimes had to find a way to make certain particularly unsavory characters or acts specially memorable. He therefore described the activities of Col. William H. Phelps, an officer of the Missouri Pacific Railroad and lobbyist for the railway interests of Jay Gould in sexual terms. "New legislators often bothered him, especially 'honest men'," wrote Steffens, "Senators who would not take money. Sometimes he 'got' them with passes, which was cheap, but not sure, so he had been compelled sometimes actually to 'rape' some men, as he did Senator Frank

Busche, of St. Louis." To get Busche's vote against a railway safety bill, Phelps "thrust a hundred dollar bill into
his pocket." After that Phelps kept Busche, like a favorite
whore, on a regular salary.[26]

Similarly, Steffens said New Jersey, with its lax corporation charter law, was "the business Tenderloin of the
United States" and charged the state with "self-prostitu-
tion." The laws required outside corporations chartered
in New Jersey to hold certain of their corporate meetings
in the state. Many men came across the New Jersey line
to hold meetings in the shabby hotels of Hoboken. "Some
of these 'hotels' were vice resorts at night, but the trusts
didn't care; they continued to use them for financial as-
signations by day." Steffens titillated his readers with
such talk, but, knowing how seriously Americans of his
generation took the challenge of "white slavery" to their
homes and families, he probably worried them, too.[27]

Beyond this, Steffens was also a story teller, using his
skill at weaving tales to remind readers that the world of
graft was not a world of abstraction. Whatever its motivation or ultimate tendency, it was peopled by human be-
ings who were arrogant, brutal, funny or afraid. The
"struggle for self-government" was often a struggle indeed, and Steffens filled his articles with dramatic dialogues. Missouri's Lieutenant Governor, John A. Lee, for
example, who had once sold his influence to the "alum
faction" in the baking powder fight, wanted to reform
and vote yes to legislation unfavorable to alum, but his
weak will withered as the alum faction's Senator Frank
Farris bought him and then humiliated him. The final
scene portrays Lee himself presiding in the state Senate:

But Senator Farris was against him, and Farris arranged it
so that, when the measure came up, there was a tie in the
Senate. At the close of the roll, when the clerk turned to
the chair for the deciding vote, Farris rose in his place. The
chamber was still; everybody was aware that a weak boodler

"wanted to reform," and that the "game was to show him
up." Lee hesitated.

"Mr. President," said Farris, pointing his finger at Lee,
"we are waiting for you."

"Nay," Lee voted, in a whisper, and the trust was left in
control for two years more.[28]

Corruption came in whispers, but it also came in
shouts. Steffens described Mark Hanna's fight to win election in the Ohio legislature to the United States Senate.
Hanna had been appointed in 1897 to fill a vacancy, and
now he wanted election in his own right. He organized
well and reposed quietly in Washington to await the outcome, but suddenly in January 1898, his enemies in the
Democratic Party and among his own Republicans rose
to threaten him. Hanna rushed home, and turned his
quiet campaign into a brawl:

Columbus was a wonderful scene. The hotels were packed,
crowds surged up and down the halls and lobbies. Wine
flowed and there were loud rows and fist fights. Legislators
were kidnapped, made drunk, and held prisoners. The wife
of one member, sent for because of her influence over her
husband, was held by one side while the other kept him hidden away in a room. Men carried revolvers and showed
them, and witnesses tell me there was really a fear of sudden
death.[29]

Yet, as in *Shame of the Cities,* Steffens also knew
when to strip an event of inessential details so that the result, though it may be a distortion of immediate truth,
represented a larger, more memorable symbolic truth.
Such was his description of Chicago's Mayor Carter Harrison's visit to Springfield, the Illinois state capital, to
present his city's case concerning utilities regulation. In
reality, Harrison spent complicated days in meetings and
discussions with politicians all over town. But Steffens
wanted only to demonstrate the power of the gas and trac-

tion corporations and point up the supplicant nature of
Mayor Harrison's visit. So he stripped the scene of everything but men and chairs. Harrison arrives at the capitol
and finds Charles T. Yerkes, Chicago's most powerful
business magnate, seated "in a chair at the head of the
stairs in the rotunda of the capitol." His lieutenants, the
Governor among them, sit in other chairs at other loca-
tions. Harrison climbs the stairs to "speak for his city,"
and Yerkes laughs. What happened beyond that is unex-
plained, but, to Steffens, it was also irrelevant. The un-
equal relationship between business and the public interest is clear enough.[30]

Steffens wrote that Yerkes "represented the American businessman." That remark suggests another stylistic
device which he had used before and was important again
for understanding Steffens's thinking: the practice of reducing principal characters to stereotypes. The appearance and behavior of people had always been an essential
element in his human interest writing, and he had sometimes reduced leading characters to stereotypes, but now,
under the pressure of his own ideas concerning the large-
scale, impersonal forces that controlled society, Steffens
made more elaborate use of stereotyping than ever before. *The Struggle for Self-Government* creates a tension
between a society corrupted and reformed by people, on
the one hand, and one developing inevitably in response
to impersonal economic necessities on the other. The tension was, of course, a part of Steffens's own unresolved
thinking. What typing did was allow him to evoke his
characters with individual names, physical presences, and
behavior while at the same time see in them enough simi-
larity so that a pattern of character, or role, emerged.
The pattern was an implicit generalization about character and could be reconciled with Steffens's more explicit
generalizing about social forces.

Concerning the character of Mark Hanna, for example, Steffens left no doubt. He was variously "the true

type of our successful men of big business," or "our ag-
gressive type of the egotist," or, simply, he was typically
American. "There are traits American which he lacked,
but taken as he stood there was not a fiber of his make-up,
not a fault, not a virtue, that is not of us." He was less
an individual than he was a *kind* of person, an example
of a category. And he behaved the way he did, not according to his own individual will but rather in response
to the primal instincts that drove everyone. Using, again,
the language of naturalism, Steffens said Hanna was not
a thinker but a "man of instincts and action." His wants
were "lusts." He did not just build a machine, he built
a "primitive machine." Together with other naturalists,
Steffens apparently believed that beneath a civilized fa-
çade, man carried a set of lower drives never quite lost
through evolution. "Hanna was building his system," he
wrote of Hanna's rise in Ohio politics and his manipulation of another boss, George Cox of Cincinnati. "Not
that he knew it. Reputed as a great organizer, Hanna
worked like a bird; all he knew was that he needed straw;
his genius lay in the sure instinct with which he found his
straw. The nest happened. Cincinnati was a branch to
build on, Cox a straw." Steffens was even willing to say
that "because Hanna was so simply instinctive, we can ex-
cuse many of his evil practices; he didn't know better." [31]
   Hanna's story, however told, was an element in the
principal subject of *Struggle for Self-Government*—the
nature of political corruption in America. But Steffens's
technique of stereotyping went beyond the articles' first
purpose to create another story which paralleled the first.
He drew many characters—especially the reformers—as
innocents who must come to terms with reality, and there
emerged around them a kind of subplot in which the chief
drama centered on discovery, knowledge and the power
that came from both. *The Shame of the Cities* had, of
course, its Joseph Folk and Hovey Clarke, ordinary citizens
whose initiation into the graft-ridden politics of the big

city leaves them at first wide-eyed and then toughens them for the fight. But the theme of innocence and discovery reached a new level in *Struggle for Self-Government*.

Among the reformers whose stories Steffens tells, almost none began as a critic or even a politician. They live private, unknowing lives as lawyers or businessmen. Some, like Robert LaFollette, who was a politician (a self-confessed "green politician"), made the mistake of going to college, which postponed their awakenings and made enlightenment itself more difficult. Others, like Tom Johnson, who became mayor of Cleveland in 1901, proved narrow business careers deliberately isolated them from broader social reality. Then comes the accident of conversion—Johnson's on a train when a newsboy sells him a copy of Henry George's *Social Problems*, LaFollette's when a Wisconsin boss offers him a bribe—and the system discovers it has raised up enemies worthy of all its power.

The man whose innocence is most frequently paraded before the reader, however, is Steffens himself. More than in *Shame of the Cities* he made himself a character in this book. He speaks more often in the first person, sits at dinner with bosses and reformers alike, and reports personal interviews at greater length. He is not consistently innocent anymore (he had seen too much for that), and he does not himself experience any single conversion. (Much later Steffens would say that the Bolshevik Revolution changed everything and almost overnight reordered his world.) Instead he poses and re-poses as a *naif* who experiences reality in the presence of his readers, hoping to instruct them even as he is himself instructed. He had adopted such poses as early as his newspaper days in the 1890s, and now he brought the technique to perfection. The best example is his evocation of a visit to a boss in his own bastion, an invitation to size up a powerful man as Steffens himself had to do. In the Ohio arti-

cle the reader climbs the stairs with the reporter to Boss
George Cox's office above a Cincinnati saloon:

A great hulk of a man sat there alone, poring over a newspaper, with his back to the door. He did not look up.
    "Mr. Cox?" I said.
    There was a grunt; that was all.
    "Mr. Cox," I said, "I understand that you are the boss
of Cincinnati."
    His feet slowly moved his chair about, and a stolid face
turned to mine. Two dark, sharp eyes studied me, and while
they measured, I explained that I was a student of "politics,
corrupt politics, and bosses." I repeated that I had heard he
was the boss of Cincinnati. "Are you?" I concluded.
    "I am," he grumbled in his harsh, throaty voice.
    "Of course you have a Mayor, and a Council, and
judges?"
    "Yes," he admitted; "but—" he pointed his thumb over
his shoulder to the desk—"I have a telephone, too." [32]

The reporter offers no ready-made conclusions but tries instead to give the appearance of sharing an experience—
not the awareness so much as the process of becoming
aware. For the transition from ignorance to knowledge
was the subject of his book's subplot.
    Innocence, Steffens seemed to believe, was always at
a disadvantage when dealing with power. "Good citizens"
could not beat "bad men" because they simply did not
know what the enemy knew. Bosses like Cox had nothing but contempt for them, and Steffens, who knew
enough about politics to know he had more to learn,
quoted Cox's dismissal of the good men with relish. Once
in 1898 Hanna wanted Cox to allow some good businessmen to "run the machine" just long enough to see Hanna
safely through election to the Senate. Cox agreed, but,
telling the story to Steffens, he said, "Who do you think
they nominated? They nominated fellers they met at
lunch." Cox called them "the dozen raw" and they failed
so miserably that all Cincinnati "came back to him, laid

itself at his feet, and he proceeded at his leisure to, what
a judge called, the 'Russianization' of Cincinnati." [33]

On the other hand, innocents who experience conversion can virtually have their will with the bosses. Knowledge toughens them and, in the case of, say, Joseph Folk,
when Steffens followed him from St. Louis to Jefferson
City, the Missouri capital, knowledge also invested a man's
very words with power. The trapping of Missouri's Lieutenant Governor John Lee was a case in point. Lee had
bribed state legislators to defeat a certain bill, but no one
could catch him. Folk, who had experienced his conversion earlier in the fight with Boss Ed Butler and was still
St. Louis's circuit attorney, investigates, and the rest is
easy. All Folk did was "gave out an interview," and Lee
confessed. When Lee changed his mind and fled the state,
"Folk gave out another interview that brought him
back." Trials followed, "dull, slow trials, which," says
Steffens, "we need not follow." The story of trials and
evidence is, in fact, really peripheral to Steffens's main
purpose, which is to point up the simple power of a newly
aware man.[34]

The Struggle for Self-Government, published in 1906,
was in style and substance a kind of logical extension of
Shame of the Cities. It sold less well than the first book—
just under one thousand copies, compared with over three
thousand for *Shame of the Cities*—but, again, the articles
it brought together had already reached a wide readership
through *McClure's Magazine*.

Upbuilders (1909)

Steffens's third and last muckraking book, *Upbuilders*, published in 1909, collected articles which had appeared between 1906 and 1908.[35] It, too, is an extension
of its predecessor. Following publication of *Struggle for
Self-Government*, Steffens became increasingly fascinated

with that book's subplot: innocence and the transforming
power of knowledge. The book takes up the stories of
five citizen-reformers: Mark Fagan, Mayor of Jersey City;
Everett Colby, State Senator from Essex County, New
Jersey; Ben Lindsey, a juvenile court judge in Denver;
Rudolph Spreckels, businessman and reformer of San
Francisco; and W. S. U'Ren, Oregon's "people's lobbyist"
and state legislator. But in Steffens's book they share so
many characteristics that they may as well be a single
character.

All but one, Rudolph Spreckels, are mild-mannered,
unassuming men who do not know they are about to
become reformers until the point of sudden confrontation
with the world of graft. Spreckels is much more the
hard-nosed businessman, but even he must discover corruption even if the discovery does not precipitate a life
crisis. Otherwise, Fagan has a "pleading, almost depen-
dent look" about the eyes, Colby is a "boy" at his election to the New Jersey legislature, Judge Lindsey is "built
like a flower," and U'Ren is known as "the pussy cat"
because of his slight figure and purring speech. Once
aroused, all of them become powerful and can defeat corrupt political veterans. Some, like Spreckels or U'Ren, win
through hard, cold politics. Others, like Fagan or Judge
Lindsey, beat the bosses in quiet, almost mysterious ways
which leave their opponents (and often the reader, too)
confounded and uncomprehending.

Steffens highlights his upbuilders' potential for enlightenment by noting that their formal schooling was
slight. They would not have to undergo Steffens's own
long process of unlearning the distortions of formal education. Fagan was better off with six months' schooling
and a long apprenticeship in a funeral parlor, while Colby
was fortunate in not learning to read until he was fifteen.
Spreckels's education, like much of Steffens's own, came
from long boyhood wanderings astride his pony.

It is clear, too, that their mildness of manner and

also their reform victories are related to a new force in
Steffens's construction of the reformer type: Christianity.
The reporter asks Fagan how he resists the subtle temptations to corruption in political life, and, after some hesita-
tion, Fagan shyly whispers, "I pray." Judge Lindsey does
not punish juvenile offenders; instead he is portrayed as a
secular evangelist working to elicit cleansing confessions
from the boys and girls who come before his bench.
"Without thinking much about it," says Steffens, "he was
putting into practice in actual life, and, of all places, in
the criminal courts, the doctrine of faith, hope, and charity." U'Ren, on the other hand, takes his inspiration from
the Old Testament and dreams of becoming, like Moses,
a Lawgiver.[36]

Steffens developed the Christian theme more fully in
a popular Christmas story published a few months before
Upbuilders appeared but written after it had appeared
in magazines. It was called "The Least of These" and was
later republished as an illustrated gift book.[37] The story
concerns a mission-worker turned jailer who reforms convicts by leaving the prison door open, trusting them in
other ways, and by generally giving them hope for redemption. His name is Bailey, and he is another of
Steffens's mild, sweet, undemonstrative men who is also
Steffens's model of the Christian who takes seriously
Christ's dictum that "inasmuch as ye did it not to one of
the least of these, ye did it not to me." He performs
menial tasks for criminals and accepts their surprising
obedience with neither shame nor pride. In "The Least of
These" there is a reporter who has to "hurt" Bailey as
he probes his humility and forces him to reveal his hidden
goodness. The reporter is a new version of Steffens himself, which he used also in some of the *Upbuilders* articles.
Whereas in *Shame of the Cities* and *Struggle for Self-
Government* he had often portrayed himself as an innocent, now he was a wise interrogator and manipulator of
men.

One hardly knows what to make of *Upbuilders*. However wise he thought he had become, Steffens's reformers with their meekness and gentle, mysteriously effective Christianity are not at all convincing. His intent was to show how powerful for good a single man could be, but when these five men win elections or strip mighty bosses of their power, they seem to do these things with no greater weapon than sincerity. One is tempted to think that in writing *Upbuilders* Steffens was responding more to Theodore Roosevelt's criticism that the muckrakers did not put enough "blue sky" in their work than to his own critical observation of life. Yet he said when *Upbuilders* was published that as he corrected the proofs he realized that the book "contains about all of the foundation of my philosophy and is written as well as I can write." [38] In any case, ten months after publication, *Upbuilders* had sold only 684 copies, and it was his least-popular muckraking book.

Steffens wrote articles and stories that were not collected in books, two of which showed that the mildness of the "upbuilders" was not his final vision of reform. An article on William Randolph Hearst, the newspaper publisher and, by 1908, a leftist presidential hopeful, and one on Eugene V. Debs, the labor leader and chief exponent of socialism, were both sympathetic to their subjects.[39] Steffens's enthusiasm for Hearst and Debs was enough to precipitate a break between him and the more conservative muckrakers.

He also prepared a series of weekly newspaper articles on the influence of special interests on the federal government to follow up and complete his work on local and state government. Editors among whom this series was syndicated in 1906, however, complained that the eleven articles were dull and didactic, possessing none of the human interest that gave life to *Shame of the Cities* and *Struggle for Self-Government*.[40]

Finally, Steffens attempted a book-length analysis of

Boston business and politics at the invitation of Boston
leaders themselves. He spent 1909 in Boston, but in the
years following, the book he contracted to write dragged
on and on and demonstrated, among other things, that
Steffens was more at home writing popular articles than
books. He never finished it, but the fact that he went to
Boston at all bore out the sense of personal engagement
which began with *Shame of the Cities* and increased
through the next two collections. Steffens's activism did
not end. In some ways it was just beginning.

4

•••

Mediator

The year 1910 was a benchmark in Steffens's personal and
professional life. It is easy to see now that his writing and
interests began thereafter to flow in new channels, and Steffens himself may have felt at the time, as 1910 changed to
1911, that his life was changing.

Josephine Bontecou Steffens, his wife of twenty
years, was ill in 1910 in a way that seemed more than
passing. Their relationship had always been ambivalent.
To Josephine, her husband's professional career was
simultaneously the object of her jealous guardianship and
also a constant reminder of her failure to realize her own
early promise. Now she seemed to be dying a little each
day, and by the first week of January 1911, she was gone.
Steffens grieved for her longer than he expected he
would, and his reading of her secret diary, filled with re-
proaches over the years of their marriage, deepened the
inevitable guilt a survivor must feel.

Three months before Josephine died another event
occurred which also suggested an end and a beginning.
For years Los Angeles had been plagued with industrial
warfare brought on by business resistance to union organization. By 1910 there was talk of a general strike. In
October a dynamite bomb exploded in the building of the
Los Angeles Times, ripping out walls and killing twenty
people. The *Times*'s publisher, Harrison Gray Otis, had
led the fight against unions and now called for the hunt-

ing down of "unionite murderers." In April 1911, police in Detroit arrested John J. McNamara, secretary of the International Association of Bridge and Structural Iron Workers, while Indianapolis police took his brother, James McNamara, into custody. The two were extradited to California where in October 1911, a year after the crime, they stood trial for murder.

Josephine's death and the McNamara trial turned Steffens away from old patterns and suggested new opportunities. He moved out of his house at Riverside, Connecticut, a home he and Josephine had loved, and he became a wanderer. Steffens's journalism had made him something of an itinerant anyway, but now he was, by choice it would appear, without a home base. He went to California, then briefly to Europe, and "home" to Greenwich Village in 1911. The years from 1914 to 1920 would find him shuttling from New York to Europe, Mexico and Russia. He attended the Paris Peace Conference of 1919 to watch the assembled powers try to end the World War. He liked Paris so much that he stayed long after the press and powers went home and seriously considered permanent expatriation.

The McNamara case engaged his attention as no other event had for years. More important, it suggested for Steffens a new role. For ten years he had been fascinated with personal life as an educational enterprise in which innocence became wisdom and wisdom became power. A single transforming experience was often the center of a given tale. If Steffens's own education took longer than most, he felt by 1910 that he had acquired knowledge, and the McNamara case now offered a chance to use the power he felt as well. He wanted to play a new, more active role in public life. Specifically, he would imagine himself a wise mediator between hostile forces—between, in the McNamara case, radical labor and a fearful, confused middle class society. Steffens felt that his contacts with both sides made him uniquely able to effect reconciliation between them, since he was born of the middle class himself and had once shared its assumptions before deciding that competitive business society must be replaced with a left-moving, cooperative society. Steffens wanted to do more than write about the Mc-Namara trial, though he did arrange a nationwide syndicate of newspapers to circulate his reporting of it. He wanted to intervene directly in the proceedings and convince each side, represented in the courtroom by the prosecution and the defense, that they must admit guilt—personal guilt for the McNamara brothers, social guilt for the business society which drove working men to extremes. Social harmony could come only from observing the Golden Rule to do unto others as you would have them do unto you.

He went to Los Angeles for the opening of the trial in October 1911, and persuaded the McNamaras (and their attorney, Clarence Darrow) that they must plead guilty if the prosecution and the court would agree to a light sentence. If the brothers admitted guilt, Steffens thought he could persuade his newspaper readers that their obvious personal guilt was no greater than the less understood social guilt of a society which abused labor and drove it to revolution. Meanwhile Steffens filled his personal correspondence with dialogues between himself and lawyers, the trial judge, business leaders and even Harrison Gray Otis, whose newspaper the McNamaras bombed. Then everything fell apart. The McNamaras pleaded guilty, but the judge turned on Steffens as a meddler and sentenced the confessed dynamiters to life in prison. Some people laughed at Steffens, and others blistered with anger. In his shame he would spend time over the rest of his life in unsuccessful attempts to obtain pardons for the men his scheme had ruined.[1]

But Steffens carried more than a sense of guilty responsibility away from the McNamara case. The new role of mediator still seemed worthwhile, and it became a part

of his life. Whenever he could, he sought to place himself
between the right and the left. He attended a radical labor rally in 1914, for example, and would remember that
the most important occurrence was his personal mediation
between the police and the radicals based upon half-re-
membered police friendships going back to the 1890's. In
other ways, too, Steffens placed himself between the society of the dying past and that of the emerging future.[2]

It was natural, then, that the mediator role became
the dominant theme in his writing. That was so even
though the volume of his work was smaller in this decade
than before. The McNamara case tarnished his reputation
among magazine editors since his role in it revealed the
important fact that his own politics were moving leftward.
Then too, the fact that he chose the Mexican Revolution of
1914–16 and the Russian Revolution of 1917 for his next
major experiments in mediation made him further suspect. Revolution seemed to Steffens an obvious demonstration of the old order's passing, and he was drawn to the
two great upheavals of the decade. But middle America—
Steffens's traditional readership—was frightened, and
editors were uneasy about his identification with revolution. Occasionally he had to agree to publish under a
pseudonym or not at all. Much of his thinking went into
private correspondence, especially during his attendance
at the Paris Peace Conference, a gathering Steffens observed as the symbol of the dying old world while he kept
an ear tuned to news from Bolshevik Russia, the symbol
of the new. Read today, those letters present a varied and
interesting consciousness of politics and personality
which offset the meagerness of his published writing.

It is also worth reporting that Steffens turned more
often to fiction than he had before. In his muckraking
phase, he wavered between narration and didacticism, but
now, as he imagined himself less a seeker after truth and
more a communicator of truth, he wanted to be a story
teller. "I think I'll do less and less of article writing

now," he told his sister Laura, in 1916, "and more fiction; the only form for the truth." [3] Political patterns,
economic relationships and the whole world of social reality impressed him chiefly as a series of discrete stories.
Each one had a moral, often painfully unsubtle. But the
fact that each tale openly illustrated some larger truth
only underscored the fact that Steffens viewed life experience as occurring in simple packages. Events seemed to
fit together with little pushing or rearrangement by the
observer, the story teller. It became a familiar pose for
Steffens to open a story with himself talking aimlessly to
a businessman or foreign politician and suddenly realize
that his companion is about to tell him a story. Then
he makes a great show of his care not to disturb the process but instead draw out and make way for the story that
has been pre-constructed for his hearing.

This concern for form is not surprising considering
Steffens's new role as mediator. His communication with
the old order depended upon his ability to make the unsettling realities of revolution and self-determination acceptable to middle class readers. In a letter to his young
nephew, Clinton Hollister, Steffens tried to explain the
paradox of his using fiction to describe reality. "I am
writing some stories, for I'm a story-teller, you know," he
wrote in 1915. "A story-teller among grown-ups is different from a story-teller among children. A boy story-teller
is a sort of liar. A man story-teller is one who has a truth
to tell and, to make it more acceptable, puts it in the form
of a lie." [4]

The story, the "truth" Steffens had to tell was that
world revolution was at hand, and his own purpose was to
mediate between the old and new worlds so as to make its
advent easier to accept. He was beyond the point where
the result of one or another election could make him
happy or depressed. That sort of success or failure occurred only in the short range, whereas real political or
economic progress was an evolutionary process of much

larger span and scope. One could resist the revolution, whose unmistakable signs Steffens thought he saw in Mexico and later in Russia, but resistance would only make its coming more painful rather than stop it. Just before he left for Mexico to observe the Mexican Revolution firsthand in November 1914, Steffens expressed this transition in his thinking in a letter to Allen Suggett, his brother-in-law and a confidant to whom he often expressed ideas he could not easily publish. He was still for LaFollette and the progressives, Steffens said, "But that is only personally. In the bigger sense I can't lose anymore; not I, myself. I'm not sure enough of what is right to put my heart into any political contest to be stabbed and stepped on. Taking the long range view I can see progress everywhere and the laws of biology and sociology work out to some other end than mine by other paths than those I have traced out." Then, aware that his thinking had come to a turning point, Steffens continued his letter in an autobiographical mode, a format that was increasingly meaningful to him:

Our purposes and Nature's get crossed; our ethics run counter to her physical laws, and so our bubbles break. But my interest now is to find out her ways, not mine, and more and more I want what she wants. Nor is this reverence or religion. It's the scientific spirit; not the scientist's; that, too, is personal and concerned with short measures. I'd like to get back to where I was when a student abroad, twenty years ago. I decided then that what we needed was an ethics and a social order founded on the laws of biology. But I turned from ethics to morals because biology hadn't laid its own foundation yet; and I studied human conduct as it actually behaved. And it has been a rich study; so rich that I often forgot my ultimate purpose. And that's why I was personal and emotional. And I'm those things yet in some degree; too much so. But at least I can see that I was nearer right at first. We can't solve economic problems with morality; it's the other way.

This idea is what I'm putting into these stories I'm

writing. For it's no use telling the thing direct. We men and
women are as little children. We must talk and be taught
in parables.[5]

Mexican Stories

Steffens published his first Mexican piece, "The
Sunny Side of Mexico," in May 1915, a few months after
returning from the first of two visits to revolutionary
Mexico.[6] He had gone there in November 1914 at a point
when normally confused revolutionary politics were chaotic. Steffens knew what other American newspaper readers did about Mexico: the thirty-five-year dictatorship of
Porfirio Diaz had been overthrown in 1911 by a reformer, Francisco Madero, who was himself overthrown
in 1913 by another dictator, Victoriano Huerta. Then,
in April 1914, President Woodrow Wilson intervened in
Mexican affairs by landing marines at Vera Cruz. Huerta
fell from power a few months later leaving Mexico and its
revolution in the hands of three rivals, Venustiano Carranza, Pancho Villa and Emiliano Zapata, each of whom
controlled some territory but no one of whom could domi-
nate the others and all of Mexico.

Steffens's arrival in Vera Cruz in November coin-
cided with the evacuation of American troops, but the
open conflict among the revolutionaries meant that Mexican politics were extremely volatile. Carranza was the
nominal president, but Villa controlled Mexico City and
Carranza had moved his government to Vera Cruz.
Meanwhile, fire, death and violence were a way of life as
first one faction, then another swept through the capital
and countryside.

Steffens remained in Mexico four months, but the
article he wrote bears no resemblance to this revolutionary chaos. "I have just had a peep into a Garden of
Eden:" he began, "a bountiful, great, warm country

where nobody need work very hard. It might be heaven. The Earth is so motherly and the sun so passionate, constant, and—so paternal that the people there can live like children." From the safety of Vera Cruz, lately occupied by United States Marines and now controlled by Carranza, the Mexican Revolution did not seem destructive, and Steffens could take a broader look at the need for revolution and hope to interpret it to readers in the United States.

Indeed, much of the article seemed designed by Steffens to establish his credentials as a mediator between the United States and the Mexican Revolution. The article, written as the personal story of his travels, shows that Steffens has contacts with all sides. He begins in New York where he has a pleasant chat with an unnamed "capitalist" worried about his Mexican investments. Then a boat bound for Vera Cruz stops first in Cuba where Steffens interviews an editor whose country is securely dominated by a much-hated United States but who is willing to talk openly to Steffens. In Vera Cruz he meets more businessmen and a Mexican soldier of fortune, and, at last, interviews President Carranza. Except in the presence of Carranza, Steffens represents himself as a wise conversationalist whose half of each dialogue is filled with unemotional common sense and gently stinging Socratic ironies. With Carranza, however, he is content to ask simple questions and accept whatever reluctant replies he gets. "He has to wait, I take it," Steffens wrote of Carranza. "He doesn't dare to speak right out; not to foreigners. His feelings are too intense; his opinions are too revolutionary; and he has been too generally—I was going to say misunderstood, but it's the other way, I think. He has been too well understood." A year later, during Steffens's second visit to Mexico, Carranza would talk more freely and even invite Steffens aboard the special train he used to tour the country as he gradually extended his control over Mexico.

What Steffens learns from the more reticent Carranza in "Sunny Side of Mexico," however, is what he already knew: that Mexico is a garden threatened by the "serpent" of foreign capital development. If its people, hungry for land and self-determination, can rid themselves of the serpent, peace can return. Steffens would use his contacts—imagined or real—with both sides to ease the progress of Carranza's revolution. This article was, in effect, the first step.

Steffens returned to Mexico in October 1915, and subsequently he published three stories and two more articles about the revolution. By this time, Carranza's forces had defeated Villa at the Battle of Celaya (April 1915) and, though Villa remained a threat in the north, Carranza largely controlled the country. The month Steffens came back to Mexico, the United States accorded Carranza's government *de facto* recognition.

He traveled more deeply into the interior than he did the first time, but what he saw left him no less convinced that the revolution was good. His fiction avoided revolutionary demands and programs, however, and focused instead on "revolutionary moments" in the lives of followers and leaders. Steffens seemed implicitly to be asking how day-to-day events of revolution changed people's values and sharpened their awareness of life and death. A year earlier, from the vantage point of Vera Cruz, Mexico seemed sleepy. Now it was alive with chaos, reckless enthusiasm, youthfulness, and sheer unpredictability. Revolution was a transforming experience, and Steffens stressed this optimistically to American readers who, reading elsewhere of Mexican blood and destruction, presumably feared the upheaval across the border.

His story "Bunk," for example, is about a youthful major in a Mexican revolutionary army who runs afoul of a faction in his own force and is sentenced to be shot at dawn.[7] While various "gringos" who are fond of him, including the story's narrator, rush around trying to pull

strings and secure his release, the boy-major tries to talk
his way out of death. Standing at last before a firing squad
he pleads and chatters about his heroic exploits, his patriotism, his aging mother. But it is all "bunk"—lies
and flattery—and his executioners are unimpressed. Then
at the last moment as the rifles are aimed he shouts in a
mad, challenging stream that he loves life and wants to
live. He insults his captors, telling them they, who are *not*
about to die, would not know what to do with a reprieve,
even a day more of life, if they were given it. He would.
He would eat, drink, love, hustle money from gringos,
everything. The roar of the rifles' volley fills the air, but
the major stands. In a moment of intense awareness of
being alive he has convinced the squad leader to order
his men to miss their mark.

Because Steffens was too heavy-handed as a fiction
writer, the existential moment is buried in mere senti-
mentality. But, subtle or not, the story's point was that
revolution could create a kind of honesty which, given
Steffens's lifelong disgust with hypocrisy and pious lies,
seemed to him no small achievement.

The revolution could, on the other hand, create a
kind of bunk of its own, though even when it involved
matters of life and death, Steffens made it seem charming rather than destructive. "The Great Lost Moment" is
a story that begins with Steffens allowing himself to be
fooled into paying a certain Major D'Alegro's debt to a
carriage driver.[8] (The illustrator of the piece as it appeared in *Everybody's* even sketched Steffens impassively
giving the driver fifty *pesos*.) But in return, D'Alegro
gives Steffens another story of the revolution.

It is, again, a story about the full, intense experience
of life compacted into a brief space of time. "I've been
wondering," says Major D'Alegro, at the edge of his tale,
"whether a man—a live one—can't crowd into a moment
—or two—as much happiness as an ordinary dub spreads

out over a lifetime." He then tells about a captain whom he ordered to execute sixteen cadets from the military academy at Chapultepec. They had resisted the revolutionary army with unusual zeal and, as symbols of the old tyranny, they must be shot. But the captain, whose emotions are overcharged with revolutionary romanticism and who has a girl friend to impress, hires a band and marches the cadets to a public square where he addresses them in florid, patriotic rhetoric before shooting them one by one. And the cadets submit not just willingly but enthusiastically, as much moved by the whole occasion as the captain. Major D'Alegro intervenes to stop the proceeding, personally disgusted and worried about how such a spectacle will be viewed by higher authority. In a matter of hours, the young captain himself stands before a firing squad and in the midst of the same crowd. His own patriotic ardor makes him as willing now to be shot as he was earlier eager to shoot. Both he and D'Alegro address the crowd, D'Alegro, deeply moved, shouting that he must be honest and confessing that he does not really support the revolution. But the crowd prefers the captain's speech with its less honest, romantic appeal to glory, patriotism and the revolution. His death is just another kind of bunk.

Here was no revolution of blood and terror, Steffens seemed to be saying. Its pace was fast and its turns of fate sudden and unpredictable, but when the revolutionaries were extreme their excesses seemed more absurd than threatening. In any case, revolution gave life an intensity and a focus which seemed its most present justification.

Steffens's fictional characterization of the Mexican Revolution was only one phase of his mediation between the revolutionaries and the American middle class. His second trip to Mexico also produced two articles, "Making Friends With Mexico" and "Into Mexico and—Out!," which attempted to present the case for revolution in a

more programmatic manner.[9] Even so, though the articles
dealt with real, named figures like Porfirio Diaz, Francisco Madero, and Venustiano Carranza, Steffens tended
to evoke them in terms of character types he had used
earlier as a muckraker. In "Making Friends With Mexico," for example, which described the progress of the
revolution from Diaz, a tool of foreign capitalism, to Carranza, Steffens's personal favorite, the principal actors are
"bosses" and "reformers" on the American model. One
of them, Francisco Madero, who led the revolution briefly
following the overthrow of Diaz in 1911, even resembles
one of Steffens's innocents. His nickname is Pancho, which
Steffens translates as "Frank." He was born to a wealthy
aristocratic family, but though they sent him abroad for
study, he had the good sense to avoid formal education
and to search for ideals "in the art schools and art
groups, among the radicals and intellectuals." Still,
Madero returned to Mexico a "dreamer," who is "not
worldly wise." He preaches political and economic democracy before crowds of workingmen and peons and soon
even leads a revolution. But when his confrontation with
hard reality comes, Madero is not transformed but killed.
Huerta and the agents of foreign capital depose and murder him. It is left to Carranza, who had tried to warn
Madero and whom Steffens said is "too knowing" to allow foreign interests to defeat the revolution, to carry on.

Both articles proposed that no matter how offensive
or outlandish the Mexican Revolution was, it was nonetheless intelligible in terms of patterns with which Americans
were already familiar. If Carranza's government is full
of petty graft and stealing, that only means "Mexico is
just now having her Tweed days." As an unfortunate
"stage of democracy," it would pass. When Carranza put
his government aboard a train and spent months constantly
moving among the Mexican people, it was "like an American political campaign" complete with whistlestops and
railway station crowds. And the analogy could be broader

than isolated comparisons. Steffens summed up the larger
commonality in "Making Friends With Mexico":

Every American carries a key to the understanding of Mexico
today. It's the story of his own city, his own state, or of the
United States in our own day. We have had our political
bosses with their political rings and business backers; corruption, incompetence, and scandal. And we have had also
our poor little reform movements with their high hopes and
their long, disappointing fights for the right against the
opposition which is able to rally behind the wrong the
churches, the press, business, the State, the machines,
the system of organized society, and, finally, the people
themselves. We have been up against it? Well, that's the
story of the Mexicans. That's our key to Mexico.

Understood in these terms Mexico seemed a little less
foreign. There were differences between the United States
and Mexico, of course—differences of environment, de-
velopmental stage, and ideals. What they shared, finally,
was the same enemy: business rule through political
bosses. A common fight, Steffens hoped, would unite the
Mexican and American people in sympathy, at least, and
turn American suspicions to friendly encouragement.

By the time these pieces were published in 1916, the
task of mediation must have seemed overwhelming.
Throughout the previous year American public sentiment
increasingly favored intervention to protect property and
investments. Then, in the first months of 1916, a series of
incidents brought the two countries close to war. Pancho
Villa, defeated by Carranza and in retreat to his northern
stronghold, suddenly turned on the United States hoping, apparently, to precipitate a war in which Carranza
would be discredited. In January, Villa boarded a Mexican train at San Ysabel and shot sixteen American pas-
sengers. In March, Villa crossed the border into New
Mexico, burned the town of Columbus and killed nine-
teen of its citizens. Within a week, President Wilson or-

dered a "Punitive Expedition" commanded by General
John J. Pershing to pursue Villa into Mexican territory.
Pershing did not catch Villa, but as the expedition
plunged deeper into Mexico, relations between the United
States and Mexico rapidly deteriorated. By May 1916,
both countries stood at the edge of war.[10]

To Steffens the situation presented another opportunity to act as mediator. He had, or thought he could
get, the confidence of politicians on both sides of the border. Villa was a "grossly illiterate, unscrupulous, unrevolu-
tionary bandit," who seemed, nonetheless, to be the Wall
Street candidate for ruler of Mexico. Steffens chose Carranza, a wealthy aristocrat who, if he was not a total revolutionary, was at least a bulwark against foreign economic
domination. Steffens had traveled aboard his train and
thought he could speak for him. On the other hand he
also knew the American bankers and oil men who tried
to control Mexico's natural resources from hotel lobbies.
Steffens imagined that these men, "the hard, bold, bad,
big rascals that like me best," kept no secrets from him
and even consulted him on the ethics of their business
deals. Beyond them were Steffens's contacts with President Wilson's cabinet, including Newton D. Baker, Secretary of War. At the first sign of trouble, Steffens stood
ready. "I think," he wrote in March 1916 as he prepared to come home, "that, maybe, I can pull off some
sort of colonial policy." [11]

The key to the American position was Wilson himself. At the height of the crisis, with almost everyone in
Washington talking of war, Steffens called on the President. Wilson would not see him, so Steffens wrote what
he later called "a silly note": "A war due to irresistible
causes is bad enough, but a war made by misinformation
is unforgivable, and I, for one, will never forgive it." [12]
The United States stood at the brink of war, he thought,
only because Wilson believed Carranza wanted a war to
boost his own sagging political fortunes. Steffens knew

Carranza better and knew he did not want war. The next
day Wilson invited Steffens to the White House and heard
him out.

In his autobiography, Steffens said Wilson listened
and then replied, "You have given me information, very
valuable information, information which prevents a war."
Steffens used the incident to establish his own centrality
in the Mexican crisis. Except for Lincoln Steffens, one is
led to believe, there would have been a second Mexican
War.[13] Nor is this point of view different from what
Steffens thought at the time. Nonetheless, it is an interpretation that grossly over-simplifies the much more complex economy of forces which made for peaceful settle-
ment of Mexican-American differences. There is no doubt
of Steffens's sincerity as a mediator; nor does one disbe-
lieve that Steffens presented himself to Wilson as he said
he did. But many more peacemakers than he surrounded
President Wilson, including especially Samuel Gompers of
the American Federation of Labor. More important, Wilson in 1916 was preoccupied with the possibility that the
United States might be drawn into the general European
war that had been raging for two years. Entanglement
with Mexico, Wilson knew, would make his European
policy more difficult. When Mexico and the United States
agreed to negotiate their differences through a Joint High
Commission in the summer of 1916, the easing of tensions
had resulted from a variety of counsels.[14]

In any case, Steffens might well have looked to one
of his own stories for a more skeptical commentary on the
nature of mediation. In July 1916, as the crisis was passing, he published "Thirty-Threed, A Tale of Our Border Today." The story had no meaning at all, he told his
sister Laura, and in fact he hoped it would counter criticism that his fiction was always pushing some secondary
point. "It's just a portrait, without significance or criticism," he said. "I simply enjoy and offer for my reader's
enjoyment a character I met." [15]

Still, read against the background of Steffens's attempt to mediate the dispute between Mexico and the
United States, the story has at least ironic interest. It deals
with an American newspaperman, Tommy Tyler, whose
nickname, "Press of the World," rather obviously broad-
ens his character into the dimensions of a whole category.
He represents "the very serious expression of the shame-
less joy of being alive and young and—an utterly irre-
sponsible, highly privileged war-correspondent, with a
reckless army in a perfectly lawless revolution." What he
enjoys most is getting himself into trouble—"a hole," he
says—so that he can get out of it again. Encamped with
the forces of Pancho Villa on the Mexican side of the
Rio Grande, Tyler advises a not-very-discerning Villa on
how to smuggle guns and ammunition through an American arms embargo. Finally he offers to mediate between
Villa and the American President by promising to persuade Wilson to lift the embargo altogether. Tyler knows
that Villa would shoot him on the spot if he suspected
he were trifling with him, but the chance to fool Villa
is too good to pass up. He has already heard a rumor that
Wilson is about to lift the embargo anyway, and knowing
that Villa could not be aware of it, he tells him he will
use his "influence" in Washington to get what Villa
wants. When Wilson does in fact raise the embargo, Villa
yells, hugs Tyler, commands everyone in his band to hug
him, and orders two freezers of ice cream to be consumed
in his honor. Tyler has the last laugh, of course, knowing
full well that Wilson's decision was born of more influ-
ences than a petition from the "Press of the World."

At the time, Steffens did not see any autobiographical
overtones in "Thirty-Threed." He believed that he stood
in the center of a major crisis that was no joking matter.
Speaking of Wilson and Carranza he said at the end of
July 1916, "Well, they both trust me now, so I'm am-
bassador for both sides, as they both know." [16]

Russian Stories

Steffens had high hopes for the Mexican Revolution, but he always said it did not make sense, not Marxist sense anyway. World revolution was supposed to begin in industrialized countries, but Mexico was backward.

So was Russia, and yet in 1917 another revolution broke out there which had a more far-reaching effect. It did not make Marxist sense either, and for Steffens it did not make sense from any point of view. A crisis in Russia, the Bolshevik Revolution became a crisis in international affairs, and, in his autobiographical memory of it, the revolution precipitated a crisis in Steffens's own personal struggle to understand human affairs. The way he would remember it ever after, the Russian Revolution was the single event that tore the last shreds of liberalism from the structure of his thinking, reorganized the structure itself, and ended forever his muckraker's expectation that democratic elections, reforms, and mere regulation of America's business life would create a happy society. That a Marxist revolution could happen in a barely industrialized country was not the only surprise: Steffens was surprised that he had held on so long to a liberalism that had been, in a sense, outdated for years without his knowing it and which needed but the shock of reality for it to crumble altogether.[17]

The shock was probably not so great as he remembered it. He said, for example, that the Bolsheviki taught him that the world was in constant evolution toward higher, more perfect forms of society. When he returned from his second trip to Russia in 1919 and remarked, "I have seen the future, and it works!" he was attempting to transform that evolutionary idea into an epigram. But the concept was hardly new to his mind. Rather, the Rus-

sian Revolution confirmed a way of looking at society that
had roots running back through at least two decades of
Steffens's writing.

Though Steffens was to spend much of the next
twenty years—the rest of his life—explaining and de-
fending the Bolshevik Revolution as good news for modern men, the striking fact about his Russian articles and
stories is their mediocrity. Between 1917 and 1924 he
wrote only six brief pieces directly concerned with the
Revolution. He wrote nothing comparable to his protégé,
John Reed's *Ten Days that Shook the World* (1919), and,
indeed, the only booklength treatment he produced was
Moses in Red (1926), a strained description of the Exodus as a revolution.

Why Steffens did not write more and better is something of a puzzle. The small volume of his work might be
explained by editors' suspicions of his politics or perhaps
by the fact that much of his energy went into nationwide
speaking tours on behalf of the Russian cause.

The low quality of the work is another question.
He made three trips to Russia, in 1917, 1919 and 1923
and, one thinks, ought to have had more to say. William
Bullitt, Steffens's companion for the second trip claimed
that when they were in Russia together Steffens spent most
of his time in their room, only rarely going into the streets
of Moscow.[18] Perhaps he did not see enough to write
about? Even if that were true (the source raises some
suspicions), Steffens's powerful imagination might have
filled in the spaces. It seems more likely that the quality
of the work was lowered by Steffens's insistence on carrying through his mediator's role.

His two-part story about the murder of Rasputin,
which *Everybody's* published in September and October
1917, is a case in point.[19] Mediating between Americans
and Russian revolutionaries required Steffens, as in the
case of Mexico, to establish his own credentials as an in-
sider. The first sentence of "Rasputin—The Real Story"

does just that. "The assassins' own story of the killing of Rasputin," he begins, "was told to me first in confidence, 'not for publication,' and I had no thought of printing it." But, since the story illustrates the character of Russia's revolutionary upheavals, it must be told.

What follows is, first, the story of Rasputin himself, a religious pilgrim who works his way into the confidence of the more fanatically religious Tsarina. Personally and morally unclean, he uses the Tsarina as the "clean center" from which he violates and conquers Russian wives, daughters, men, and the Tsar. Next is the story of the noblemen's plot to murder him by enticing Rasputin to a house in Petrograd where, on the night of December 31, 1916, they poison and shoot him to death.

Ostensibly, the point in recounting Rasputin's story is to explain and justify the overthrow of the Tsar to an American readership presumably puzzled by that and other news from Russia. So Steffens laces his tale with what the editorial introduction to Part One calls "astonishing parallels from our own American life." They were hardly astonishing, however, to anyone familiar with Steffens's earlier attempts to explain other countries' politics by reference to American models. Tsar Nicholas, for example, was just another "boss" like Boss Cox of Cincinnati. He was strong only as long as the special interests (banks, privileged corporations, vice rings) tolerated him. When Cox fell from power in 1911 it was a "provisional government" that deposed him, a fact which Steffens expected his readers to find meaningful when they read now in 1917 about the abdication of Nicholas II and the establishment of a new Russian Provisional Government. What Rasputin did was to disrupt the "system" by placing himself between the Tsar and his needed supporters among the "special interests." Rasputin had to die, then, and so did the interests' faith in the Tsar and Tsarina. When the Revolution came, nothing could save the royal family. Americans had seen it before.

The parallels Steffens drew between American and Russian society were "astonishing" only in their absurdity. As an attempt to explain the complex nature of Russian society and its Revolution they were facile and serve, when read today, to call into question not just Steffens's powers of observation but also his judgment.

In any case, lest this summary over-represent the space devoted to Steffens's "argument," it must be noted that the bulk of the articles merely exploit the melodrama of Rasputin's rise and especially his fall. It was as though Steffens feared readers were bored by Russian news and thought his mediator's role could not begin before he enticed them with a lurid but otherwise irrelevant tale about a dirty old man, his sexual perversity and his brutal execution at the hands of frightened gentlemen conspirators. But this tale finally overwhelms the larger point about the origins and progress of the Russian Revolution.

From the start, for example, Steffens makes it clear that the story is more important than the didactic point. He calls it a "nature-made melodrama" to emphasize, as he had in Mexico, that life presents itself as a series of stories possessed, without interpretation, of their own integrity. And if Rasputin is a central character, he is matched by "the beautiful young noblewoman," the nameless leader of the courageous conspiracy whose identity Steffens vows courageously to protect. Whoever she is, she is highborn and pure, and Steffens likes the thought that she must be touched, literally and figuratively, by the foul Rasputin and must be touched as well by Rasputin's murder, however just. Steffens admires her, too, because, unlike the "reckless dandies who set out to kill him [and] came back innocent and appalled," the duchess is wise and knowing: she is unafraid to bait the murderous trap with her own person.

Less melodramatic but equally obvious in its intent is a short story, "Midnight in Russia," which *McClure's*

published six months later in May 1918.*[20] It begins,
familiarly, with an American reporter being told a tale.
A young Russian Jew comes to his hotel room in Moscow
one night to tell his life story; he chose a reporter because he knows reporters are hard-nosed men who have a
better chance at getting and telling the Truth.

The boy says he was born in Russia and grew up in
constant fear of the pogroms—brutal, terrorizing attacks
against Jews. Dreaming of the liberty he could not have
in Russia, he emigrated to the United States. But America
was no more free than the old country, a fact his life in
New York City made him aware of every day. Corruption
and vice in American business and politics mocked his
dream of freedom, so when the Great War broke out in
1914, he returned to Russia to fight patriotically, at least,
for the Czar. His longing for liberty was still strong when,
in 1917, the Revolution began and the boy at last found
an uncorrupt cause.

Steffens fashions the boy himself as his mediator,
conveniently endowing him with experience in both Russia and America as well as in the old order and the new.
If anyone knows how things are, he does.

One of the things the boy teaches the reporter is the
central meaning and use of the revolutionary mob. Nothing, perhaps, was more unsettling to Americans observing the Russian Revolution—or any revolution—than the
unpredictable presence of a mob in the streets. Steffens
wanted to allay their fears, but the interpretation he offers through his young informant is embarrassingly sentimental.

The boy says the mob is the people, the real rulers of
Russia. One sees them roaming in their hundreds through

* S. S. McClure, under whose sponsorship Steffens first emerged as
a muckraker, no longer had anything to do with *McClure's*, having
lost control of the magazine in 1912.

the streets late at night. They stop before a government office or an official's home and demand with their brooding silence explanations and changes. They are slow and they do not understand the details of government policy, but when something is "wrong," they know it in a deep, intuitive sense. Governments, formal and capable of corruption, are bad. It was the Tsarist *government* which promoted the pogroms. The mob is, therefore, in no hurry to turn power over to a new government, says the boy. It is itself a kind of welcome direct democracy which does not need more structure or form than it already has.

Listening to this, Steffens as narrator realizes that the mob's virtue (and the boy's) is its lack of formal education. That theme, familiar in his writing, is one among several allusions Steffens makes to his own life experience. His Jewish hero is also a reminder of his interest in Jewish culture during his newspaper days in the 1890's, and his character's knowledge of New York corruption comes from that period in his life, too. The boy had come a long way, and so had Steffens, in his thinking at least. In using the young Jew as a vehicle to mediate between the Russian Revolution and the American middle class, Steffens was at the same time drawing upon images from his own past to explain what was happening to himself. The story is weak from an aesthetic point of view, but its biographical significance is unmistakable.

Steffens's romantic evocation of the revolutionary mob was repeated in "The Rumor in Russia," an essay the *Nation* published in December 1918 and which is probably the most absurd piece he ever wrote.[21] Drawing partly on the optimistic Christianity he used in *Upbuilders* and in "The Least of These," Steffens was also searching for another voice in a continuing effort to interpret Russia to America. The Russian Revolution could be understood as "nature-made melodrama," as in the tale of Rasputin, or as a remedy for an international pattern of corruption, as in "Rasputin" or "Midnight in Rus-

sia." But writing now under the pseudonym "Christian,"
Steffens argued that the Bolsheviki were doing nothing
less than preparing the Kingdom for the second coming
of Christ.

There was nothing tongue in cheek about "Rumor in
Russia." And if it is to be read as metaphor, the essay's
length and detail stretch it beyond even metaphorical use.
The whole is cast in a King James Bible rhetoric which
collapses when, at one point, Elihu Root, chairman of the
American Commission to Russia and once Secretary of
State, is identified as the speaker in the sentence, " 'How
came it,' said one, marveling, 'why was it that with no
Government and no police there was order in Russia?' "
The answer to that question was, of course, that the Revolution was fueled not by vengeance or even reckless
exuberance but by a vision of the millenium. Through
generations "spent dreadfully on dull watch, peering and
listening into the stupid stillness of their frozen Northern
night," Russian peasants listened at last to two voices, the
priest preaching of Christ and the propagandist heralding
the Revolution. The peasant reconciles them. " 'Christ
is coming, as the priest says. And as the revolutionist says,
Heaven is coming also; and first. But neither will come
until there are wars and rumors of wars, and we, the
people, have raised up the Revolution which is to prepare
His way.' "

By the time this was published, Steffens had gone to
Paris to witness firsthand the efforts of the powers to reas-
semble the world after the breakage of the Great War. It
was a special privilege not allowed to all journalists, but
he left on November 1918 with special help from Colonel
Edward House, Woodrow Wilson's adviser and Steffens's
friend.

To be in Paris in 1919 was to be present at what
seemed the most exciting, hopeful moment in history.
War had destroyed the old world, many thought, and the
idealistic American President, Woodrow Wilson, was there

to create a new one. Steffens was skeptical, but the Peace
Conference made him feel nevertheless like an actor on
the stage of great events. Colonel House was listening to
him and seemed to bring him close to Wilson. Other reporters not only knew him but lionized him, for his reputation had made Steffens, in his biographer's phrase,
a journalist "to whom other journalists rendered accounts." [22]

Three months after Steffens arrived in Paris his
chance to do more than feel like one of the principals
came. William C. Bullitt, a young American diplomat, had
been asked to make a secret and unofficial fact-finding visit
to Russia, and he wanted Steffens to go along.

Since Steffens's last trip to Russia, much had hap-
pened: The Bolsheviki, led by Vladimir Lenin and Leon
Trotsky had seized power from Alexander Kerensky's Provisional Government in November 1917. Three months
later, in March 1918, Lenin signed the Treaty of Brest-
Litovsk with Germany and withdrew Russia from the
World War. Four months after that, in June, French,
British and American troops landed at the Baltic port of
Archangel to support the anti-Bolshevik Russian forces engaged in a civil war with Lenin's group. When the World
War came to an end the following November, the Allied
intervention was still in progress, and Russia, unrepre-
sented at the Paris Peace Conference, was very much at
odds with the great powers that *were*.

Various schemes for making contact with the Bolsheviki and ending hostilities had come to nothing when the
United States and Britain proposed what became known
as the "Bullitt Mission." Steffens's role fit his self-image
perfectly. Bullitt needed Steffens to vouch for him, to be
the go-between who because of his contacts with Colonel
House and his known Bolshevik sympathies would be
trusted by both sides. So it was that Steffens undertook
yet another mediation effort not just between two coun-

tries, as in the case of the Mexican Revolution, but between the old order and world revolution.[23]

Steffens and Bullitt left Paris secretly on February 22, made their way to Petrograd two weeks later, and from there went to Moscow where they met and interviewed Lenin himself. Steffens's account of the four-week trip is his "Report on the Bullitt Mission to Russia," addressed to William Bullitt and intended for private circulation among top Allied policy makers. Eventually the document went to the Senate Foreign Relations Committee, which printed it as a government document, but it also found its way to the *Nation,* which published it October 4, 1919.

Steffens wrote his Report immediately following his return from Russia on March 25, but he already knew much of what he would say before he left Paris. Bullitt said Steffens was fashioning his famous epigram, "I have seen the future, and it works" on the way to Petrograd, long before they met the Bolsheviki.[24] And, as noted earlier, once they arrived, he claimed that Steffens spent more time in their room than he did in the streets. But Steffens did interview Lenin and brought back an impression of the Bolshevik leader that would be new if not congenial to the Western imagination.

Steffens's Report makes five points, of which the first is, "I think the Revolution there is ended; that it has run its course." [25] The flatness and finality of this assertion was calculated to cut off the hopes of those policy makers in Paris who thought the anti-Bolshevik reaction might yet produce a government more congenial to Western interests. Internal opposition had all but ceased, Steffens claimed, and continued outside intervention only drove other factions closer to the Bolsheviki. But Steffens's certainty that the Revolution was over was also designed to calm the fears of anyone who worried about the instability and unpredictability of revolution. Changes, reac-

tions, advances will surely come, he said, but they will
be "regular," "parliamentary."

The list of the Revolution's social achievements might
warm the heart of the staunchest conservative:

Certainly, the destructive phase of the Revolution in Russia
is over. Constructive work has begun.

We saw this everywhere. And we saw order, and though
we inquired for them, we heard of no disorders. Prohibition
is universal and absolute. Robberies have been reduced in
Petrograd below normal of large cities. Warned against
danger before we went in, we felt safe. Prostitution has dis-
appeared with its clientele, who have been driven out by the
'no-work-no-food law,' enforced by the general want and the
labor-card system. Loafing on the job by workers and sabo-
tage by upper-class directors, managers, experts, and clerks
have been overcome. Russia has settled down to work.

Steffens's second point was that the Revolution was
spontaneous, unexpected, even by Lenin himself. "This is
not a paper thing; not an invention," he said. That made
for some unfortunate excesses, of course, like the Red Terror, of which Lenin and the Bolsheviki were ashamed, but
its spontaneity also implied that the Revolution could not
be put down. Its time had simply come.

Third, the Bolsheviki have temporarily sidestepped
the matter of political democracy—a traditional goal for
revolution—and have aimed instead at a more total economic democracy. Worker control of economic institutions, "democracy in the shop, factory, business," must
come before political democracy can have any meaning.
Steffens's admission of the new Russia's political absolutism was as stark as any critic's charge: "The present Russian government is the most autocratic government I have
ever seen. Lenin, head of the Soviet government, is farther
removed from the people than the Czar was, or than any
actual ruler in Europe is." Yet that fact only masked the
more fundamental democratization of industry and income, the groundbase of politics.

Lenin attracted Steffens as strong leaders often had. Robert LaFollette, William Randolph Hearst, and the whole collection of tough-talking bosses from his muck-raking days all had a singlemindedness Steffens liked. Lenin now joined them, though the Bullitt Mission Report does not give him much space. "Lenin has imagination," one learns. "He is an idealist, but he is a scholar, too, and a very grim realist."

Steffens interviewed Lenin, but Lenin's character in the Report is cool and pale ("Lenin was a statistician by profession") beside the account Steffens would give of him later in *Moses in Red* (1926). "When I asked Lenin officially about the Terror," Steffens remembered in *Moses* from the 1919 interview, "he whirled on me fiercely."

"Who wants to ask us about our killings?" he demanded.

"Paris," I said, meaning, as he well understood, the Peace Conference.

"Do you mean to tell me that those men who have just generaled the slaughter of seventeen millions of men in a purposeless war are concerned over the few thousands that have been killed in a revolution which has a conscious aim: to get out of the necessity of war and—and armed peace?"

He stood a moment facing me with his blazing eyes, then quieting down, he said:

"But never mind, do not deny the Terror. Don't minimize any of the evils of a revolution. They occur. They must be counted upon. If we have to have a revolution, we have to pay the price of it." [26]

For obvious reasons, however, the Report avoided this sort of characterization and emphasized the quiet, dispassionate, orderly side of Lenin's character.

Steffens's fourth point stressed the totality of the Revolution. Lenin had uprooted institutions and obliter-ated the most common assumptions and relationships in Russian life. The old political system was "dark, crooked, and dangerous," but the poorest and the richest Russians had "groped around in it" all their lives. The wealthy knew which officials to bribe for one concession or another, and the poor knew how to haggle for goods in a market of scarcity and competition. Now the old society and its corruption were gone, but so also was its familiarity, and Steffens portrayed the Russian people as wandering in a helpless "confusion of mind" that was worse ("I mean this") than the hunger, cold, and death which they also suffered.

But Steffens's fifth and last point was that, as complete and permanent as Lenin's revolution was, it cannot be acceptable to the powers assembled at the Paris Peace Conference. Neither will the Russian proposal for peace with the Allies. The men of Paris will continue to think the specter of Bolshevism will pass and, wedded to that assumption, they will continue to make war.

This thought comes at the end of Steffens's Report, but there is reason to believe he knew the Russian proposal and, indeed, the Bullitt Mission report would be rejected even before he began writing. Bullitt cabled the Russian proposal to Paris on March 16, and he and Steffens returned there themselves on the 25th. Bullitt was to see Wilson the next day, but the President broke the appointment, pleading a "headache." Steffens, meanwhile, started his draft, but the diplomatic atmosphere was chilly. He finished by April 3 and sent his Report "to the top," yet it cannot have surprised him when the Allies let the Russians' April 10 deadline pass without a reply to their proposal. Evidently they believed the White opposition could still beat Lenin. On April 16, David Lloyd George, the British Prime Minister, denied in Parliament any prior knowledge of the Bullitt Mission.

This turn of events ought to have been depressing, but Steffens, sure that Allied rejection would make a general European revolution inevitable, was unperturbed. He simply changed the focus of his mediation. If his personal

diplomacy was unavailing, he could still interpret what he
had seen to the larger public.

His Report was probably crafted with exactly that in
mind. He paid as much attention to its style as to its content. "It is short," he wrote to a friend, "but I took a lot
of time to write it. I wanted to make it easy to read and
effective." [27] Ostensibly, the Report is addressed to Bullitt, who headed the mission, but, near the end, after summarizing his impressions, Steffens clearly separates his
function as a *publicist* from Bullitt's as a diplomat: "That
is the message you bring back, Mr. Bullitt. It is your duty
to deliver it. It is mine to enforce it by my conception of
the situation as it stands in Russia and Europe today."

Given his intentions, Steffens's Report did not long
remain in Bullitt's hands alone. By September 1919, it
was read in hearings of the Senate Foreign Relations
Committee and then released by the Committee and
printed as a government document. On October 4, the
Nation published it to a wider readership and it took its
place among Steffens's several attempts at sympathetic explanation of the Russian Revolution.

Moses in Red (1926)

Moses in Red was Steffens's last attempt to interpret
the Russian Revolution to its middle class enemies. A book-
length retelling of the Old Testament story of Israel's
Exodus from Egypt, it proposed that the ancient Israelites' progress from slavery to the promised land was a
revolution, indeed, the archetype of *all* revolutions, including the two he had most recently witnessed. The Old
Testament, cherished among Jews and Christians alike,
seemed a good vehicle to carry Steffens's argument that
revolution is both natural and legitimate. But the book
gave full voice to a more specific theme that Steffens had

been turning over in his mind for some time: the idea
that the first generation of revolutionaries—or, in this
case, the first generation of the Exodus—is too steeped
in pre-revolutionary culture to realize and accept their own
revolutionary vision. Their children may pass over into
the promised land, but they must remain behind.

Moses in Red is probably the least known of Steffens's books. It was issued by an obscure publisher, Dorrance & Co., and, to make matters worse, a warehouse
fire destroyed all but about 400 copies. "The *Moses* is
making no stir; it's not read, I take it," he wrote to his
friend Jo Davidson a few months after it was published.[28]
By then Steffens was deeply engaged in writing his *Autobiography*, a book which, when it was published, would
not even mention *Moses in Red*. Only its reprinting in
Ella Winter's and Herbert Shapiro's *The World of Lincoln
Steffens* (1962) recovered it from more than thirty-five
years of obscurity.

Needless to say, *Moses in Red* does not offer a mere
paraphrase of the Exodus. It does follow the story of
Moses and the Israelites as narrated in the books of Gen-
esis, Exodus, Leviticus, Numbers, and Deuteronomy, but
the narrative is laced throughout with Steffens's own commentary and analogues to modern revolution. The Penta-
teuch's tale of Israel's enslavement in Egypt, Moses' origins and his assumption of leadership, the flight from
Pharaoh, and the forty-years' wandering in the wilder-
ness is retold to obviously new purposes.

Steffens is explicit in identifying religious characters
with modern, secular categories:

The narrative follows the course of a typical revolution. Let
Jehovah personify and speak for nature; think of Moses as
the uncompromising Bolshevik; Aaron as the more political
Menshevik; take Pharaoh as the ruler who stands for the
Right (the conservative "evolutionist"), and the children of
Israel as the people—any people; read the Books of Moses
thus and they will appear as a revolutionary classic.[29]

Much of Steffens's reasoning is "after the fact" in nature, and his account is a large, unproved metaphor. Still, his point was at least clear if it was not convincing: God (Nature) wants progress toward utopia. Anyone who resists must fall, whether it be Pharaoh (the Right) or the Israelites (the people) themselves. The revolution in Egypt began *not* with Moses but with Pharaoh, who refused to grant Moses' peaceful petition. Despite Jehovah's repeated threats and intimidations, Pharaoh resists and therefore provokes a violent upheaval. All this fit Steffens's definition of revolution: "Revolutions, like wars, are social-economic explosions due to human (political) interference with natural (and, therefore, divine) laws and forces which make for the gradual growth or constant change called evolution." [30] It is not revolutionaries who start revolutions but those who resist nature.

Steffens's style is often an imitation of King James Bible rhetoric but it is not so bad as in his earlier essay, "The Rumor in Russia." For dramatic effect and to show that the Israelites' behavior was not unlike that of modern revolutionaries, he inserts here and there words from the vocabulary of contemporary upheaval. Thus, Moses is a "labor leader;" God and Moses hatch a "conspiracy" against Pharaoh; Moses' speeches are "demogogic;" God encourages the Israelites to "loot" Egypt as they leave; God "sabotages" Egypt's production; and God institutes a "Red Terror" first against the Egyptians and then against backsliders among His own people.

The story's dramatic highpoint, however, comes at the end when Jehovah, exasperated with the faithlessness of his flock, bars their entry into the promised land. Their children may pass over, and two of the elders, Joshua and Caleb, but all the rest, including Moses himself, must die. God summons Moses to Mount Nebo where he can see the land he cannot finally experience.

Steffens thought this bitter culmination of the Exodus the most meaningful event in the whole tale. He read it as a commentary on the fate of any revolutionary generation. They could envision and work toward the better life, but because they were also rooted in the old culture, they could not accept or enjoy the new. Indeed, God (Nature) must put them to death, and he titled this penultimate section of *Moses in Red* "The Slaughter of the Grownups." In the years following the Russian Revolution, Steffens had met leftists like Emma Goldman who had been to the Soviet Union and disliked what they saw. He was partly writing his book for her and her generation, explaining, in a patronizing tone, that the fault was not the Russians' but theirs.

That generation was also his generation, of course, and Steffens was writing about his own condition, too. In fact he had known well before the Russian Revolution that social dreamers never seemed to live long enough to see their plans through. "From Moses down through Jesus to Henry George and yourself," he wrote as early as 1909 to his idealistic friend, Tom Johnson, Mayor of Cleveland, "no great leader has ever realized himself the dream that inspired him. What is more, the greater, the truer, the more inspired his vision, the more generations it has taken to achieve his heaven." [31]

The Russian Revolution brought these thoughts to mind again, and so, thereafter, did a re-reading of the Old Testament. In 1923 Steffens made his third trip to Russia, this time accompanied by Senator Robert F. La-Follette. He returned with the impression that the new Russian was best expressed in its young men and women whose memories and roots in the old culture were small compared with their motivation and experiences in the new.

Steffens's story "Neps," which the *Transatlantic Review* published in February 1924, made this point in fictional terms. With some degree of sympathy, he portrays a post-Revolution generation gap between a sad old Russian revolutionary and her much happier children. Anticipating the *Moses* theme, she says:

There is no hope for us, they say. We are not fit for the kingdom of heaven. Therefore, Communism has to wait for us to die and for the new generation to grow up and bury us, and our habits, customs, ideas, and ideals. And they take care of the new generation. They go after the children. And they get the children.[32]

Steffens's *own* sense of being able to envision the future but not participate in it may explain why he never became actively involved in communist organizations. He supported communism and the Soviet Union with his pen through the remaining years of his life, but he never wanted to live in Russia and could never bring himself to join the American Communist Party.

As a final comment on *Moses in Red*, it may be worth saying that the problem of the revolutionary generation is also the problem of the mediator, which was, of course, Steffens's own persona after 1910. Moses was a mediator between God and the Israelites and between the Israelites and Pharaoh. A Jew raised as an Egyptian prince and also chosen by Jehovah to participate in divine events, Moses knows all worlds and can explain them to each other. Steffens knew the two worlds of his day, but, quite apart from the question of Steffens's and Moses' relative success as mediators, that stance itself, however useful it was, precluded a transit from one world to the next. Justin Kaplan has suggested that in his characterization of Moses, Steffens may have discovered at the same time the very real limitations of mediation.

The question recurs: why did Steffens write nothing on revolution of lasting value? He supposed the Russian Revolution to have revolutionized his thinking, yet his best writing, *The Shame of the Cities* and his *Autobiography*, lies on either side of the revolutionary decade.

The answer may be that Steffens became too self-conscious a mediator between the old world and what he supposed must be the new. He invested too much energy in the search for a new literary format and too little in the standard journalism, laced with human interest, that had served him well before. Once he began his *Autobiography* in the next decade he would rediscover his natural gift for story-telling and combine it with a philosophy of life and long experience in the world, including its recent revolutions, to produce his greatest work.

5

•••

Autobiographer

Writing *The Autobiography*
of Lincoln Steffens (1931)

Much of Steffens's life in the 1920s and 1930s focused
upon his *Autobiography*—its composition, its publication
and its public reception. Though his thinking had over the
years often been cast in an autobiographical mode, one
can still say that the idea to write a formal autobiography
came from events, mostly personal, which opened this last
period in Steffens's life.

The first event was meeting Ella Winter. In 1919, not
long after he returned from Russia with William Bullitt,
Steffens received an invitation to dinner from Felix Frankfurter, borne by Frankfurter's twenty-one-year-old secretary, Ella Winter. Steffens was fifty-three that year, but
he fell in love with her more deeply, perhaps, than with
anyone before. They lived together and traveled for five
years and then, in 1924, when Ella discovered she was
pregnant, they married.

It was her youth that attracted him, and, despite
the fact that she had already studied at the London School
of Economics, she became his protégé as much as his wife.
Steffens had adopted young people before, playing mentor to his sisters' children and to young Harvard graduates like Walter Lippmann and John Reed. He taught
them from the text of his own life, and at first Ella, whom

he called "Peter," was no different from the others as he
explained how he had shaken off the formal disguises
with which teachers and officials cloaked reality. But during their courtship of long walks through the streets of
Paris and London he spelled it out to Ella Winter in more
detail, explaining his life to her as a series of stories—
stories about his boyhood and pony, his student days in
Germany, and his muckraking tour of American cities.
Strolling with Ella, Steffens continued increasingly to
structure his life.[1]

The birth of their son, Pete Stanley, in 1924 was
the second event which led Steffens to his formal *Autobiography*. He had thought about writing in 1922 when
Glenn Frank, editor of *Century Magazine* offered him
$750 per chapter to serialize his life story. And, though
he started to put his thoughts in order in the summer of
1924, it was not until Pete was born that he began writing seriously. He watched as Pete changed from a baby to
a toddler and, one morning, told Ella, "I think I can start
my life now." [2]

The birth of his son made him think about youth
again, but, more than that, it made him think about his
own youth. Ella Winter said in *her* autobiography that
Steffens saw his own childhood recapitulated in Pete's and
resolved to raise his son with none of the illusions and
broken promises he had known. But suspecting, perhaps,
that at the age of fifty-eight he might not live very far
into Pete's life, he wanted to leave his *Autobiography* as a
personal testament and guide. Writing had its ups and
downs, but when it was going well it was often because
he was thinking of Pete. "I am working in a new mood,
less serious, more humorous, telling big things merrily,"
he wrote Ella's mother in 1929. "Pete's fault, I think. I
have got to imagining him reading some day his daddy's
life, so I am telling him the things I do want him to know
in the spirit in which I would have him take life. No
reverence, some fear but not much respect for law and

the conventions; how easy it is to play and win at the game." [3]

The third event which helps explain the origins of Steffens's *Autobiography* was the Russian Revolution of 1917. And since the Revolution was interwoven with the World War and the Paris Peace Conference, the one event broadened in Steffens's mind to include nearly a decade of catastrophes and new hopes. In some ways the Revolution inspired Steffens's *Autobiography* as much as more personal events did. The Revolution obviously filled him with enthusiasm, but, as noted earlier, Steffens sought in vain for a vehicle suited to carrying his formulation and defense of it. Publishers were not interested in *Moses in Red*, and other pieces seemed ineffective, too. "I don't seem to be able to state my truths so that they'll be accepted," Ella remembered him saying once. "I must find a new form." [4] The *Autobiography*, though hardly a polemic, was the answer, seeming to arrange his life superficially at least as a progress toward the certainty of a new, revolutionary world.

But the case can easily be overstated. The chief exponent of the view that Steffens's *Autobiography* is significant mainly as an argument for communism is the oft-cited 1954 essay by Granville Hicks called "Lincoln Steffens: He Covered the Future." Hicks, a young leftist social critic in the 1930s and, in time, the editor of Lincoln Steffens's letters, knew that Steffens did not "preach communism" in the *Autobiography*. But he remembered nonetheless that for his generation "the book had one special importance: it showed that there was a strictly American path to communist conclusions. . . ." [5]

The assumption appears plausible, given the time of the *Autobiography*'s publication and Steffens's persistent and, finally, embarrassing defense of Stalinist Russia even when friends whom he once trusted, such as Max Eastman, warned about Stalin's mindless repression and the beginnings of his terrible purges. One must recall, however, that Steffens's autobiographical intentions antedate both the formal writing of the *Autobiography* and the Russian Revolution. Letters, articles, and stories written over a lifetime show him self-consciously attentive to the themes of innocence, disillusion and "unlearning." And often the *Autobiography* seems more concerned with the *process* by which Steffens moved through these levels of consciousness than the specific goal at the end.

In any case, communism was only one goal. Revolution was important to him, but he liked Mussolini as much as Lenin and Henry Ford as much as either dictator. What communism, fascism, and American business efficiency shared was a rationalized—Steffens would say "scientific"—society. That was the real challenge to the old, moralistic, corrupt world.

Steffens worked on the *Autobiography* from 1924 to 1930. But, if it was the most important activity in these last years, it was not the only one. He also wrote *Moses*, of course, as well as a series of very brief fables and some articles about fatherhood at sixty. His travels, including another trip to Russia in 1923, continued and so did his expatriation. He and Ella and Pete lived on the Italian Riviera from 1924 to 1927, first in Sam Remo and then in a villa in Alassio, enjoying life *"en famille"* as he put it. In 1927, however, Steffens decided to return to California. The family settled in Carmel, a writers' and artists' colony near San Francisco whose residents included the poet Robinson Jeffers and whose visitors included a variety of American and international literati. The Steffenses called their house "The Getaway" and near the road placed a sign, "Positively No Visitors Before Four P.M." But that prohibition did not deter favorite callers, and, indeed, in Steffens's very last years a stream of friends and acquaintances insured continuing contact with the world he had once widely traveled. During his last years at Carmel he also wrote a regular column for three local newspapers: *The Carmelite* (1928–32), *Paci-*

fic Weekly (1932–4) and *Controversy* (1934). One of
them was headed "Lincoln Steffens Speaking," and that
became the title of his last book, a collection of columns
and other occasional pieces which came out in 1936, the
year he died.[6]

Whatever else he was doing, however, writing the
Autobiography and, after it was published, observing its
reception were his principal occupations in the 1920s
and 1930s. He started thinking about it seriously in the
summer of 1924, but despite the fact that the autobiographical theme had always been strong in his thinking,
the beginnings of the formal work were halting and uncertain. He had often rehearsed the meaning of his childhood but was stumped for details. "I find that my mind
of itself is brooding over the *Life* and already wants to
know some things I do not remember," he wrote his sister Laura in the fall. "When did we move from San
Francisco to Sacramento, from Second Street to between
Sixth and Seventh, from there to K at Sixteenth? When
did I get my pony, when the colt from Col. Carter, when
did I go to St. Matthew's School?" Within a year he was
writing happily, had finished four chapters and acquired
an editor in Marie Howe, wife of Frederick Howe, an
old friend whose own *Confessions of a Reformer* (1925)
was to become a small autobiographical classic. Before
long, word was out that Steffens was writing his story and
he found the world was still interested in him, for friends
offered advice ("No more ideas, Steff," pleaded August
F. Jaccaci. Just "stories, your actual experience; no in-
terpretations"), and publishers offered contracts.[7]

Then, in the middle of 1926 the work slowed as he
reached the place where he had to write about Josephine.
He had been engaged to another girl, Gussie Burgess,
when he met and secretly married Josephine, and the
memory of that time called up the more general ambivalence he knew was a flaw in his character. "I want someone with me; I want to be alone; I want to travel; I want

to stay home," he wrote to Laura. It took weeks to get
over that chapter. The muckraking chapters went well for
a time, but finally they bored him, and he found it hard
to recall the mindset of those years. "How can I put my
heart into something with which I no longer agree?" he
asked Ella. So the pace of writing ebbed and flowed over
six years. He signed a contract with Harcourt, Brace and
Company, but the publisher announced the *Autobiography* as forthcoming for two or three years before Steffens turned in his bulky manuscript. At the start of the
last year he wrote to Marie Howe, "I must be half through
my *Life*, but it's fierce; how long I did live." Finally in
the summer of 1930 he and Ella left Carmel, she for a
trip to Russia, Steffens for an extended visit with his
friend Jo Davidson, a sculptor, in France. That August,
at Bêcheron, Davidson's estate, Steffens finished his
work.[8]

The book was published in two volumes in April
1931. The Great Depression was a year old by that time,
however, and Steffens worried about how well his autobiography would do at $7.50 per set. The first edition
sold out in ten days, but by midsummer, sales slumped.
Then in the fall the Literary Guild combined the two volumes as one and made it the special selection for October
at $3.75. Sales climbed again. A year following its first
appearance, copies of the first edition were reportedly sell-
ing for $11 to $25. Lecture invitations began to multiply,
too, and Steffens was pleased to hear that his life story
was being read not only by his own generation but by
young people who knew nothing about the era. He had
feared recently that in the public mind his best work had
been accomplished long ago and that his last years would
be his most barren. The *Autobiography* erased that fear.
"I guess I'm a success!" he told Ella. "I guess I'll go down
in history now." [9]

By the time Steffens wrote his life, autobiography
had achieved the status of a genre which had its own

conventions. Augustine's *Confessions* (400 A.D.) is usually counted the first true autobiography, and then, after
an irregular development from the fifth century to the
eighteenth century, a "classical age" of autobiography
emerged. The autobiographies of Benjamin Franklin, Jean-
Jacques Rousseau, Edward Gibbon, William Wordsworth
and Johann Wolfgang von Goethe established the dimensions and responsibilities of the genre.

What is an autobiography? Perhaps Roy Pascal's formulation is best.[10] First, an autobiography presents an
individual life as *historical movement*, which makes it different from a philosophical self-portrait such as that written by Boethius or found in Friedrich Nietzsche's *Ecce
Homo* (1889, 1908). Second, though autobiography focuses on the *self*, the real subject is the self in obvious
relation to the *outside world*, which must be evoked in
equal balance with the self. Autobiography assumes that
"the self comes into being only through interplay with the
outer world." An autobiography, then, differs from a
memoir or reminiscence, which directs the reader's attention to the author's acquaintances. Third, autobiography demands the shaping of life into a coherent story.
There must be, in other words, an *organizing principle*
which the autobiographer chooses according to his current philosophy, stage or sense of achievement in life. For
"in every case," writes Pascal, "it is his present position
which enables him to see his life as something of a unity,
something that may be reduced to order." So an autobiography is different from a succession of diary entries,
for example, which presents a series of vantage points and
organizing principles rather than a single one.

Up to Steffens's time, the two seminal works of Amer-
ican autobiography were, perhaps, Benjamin Franklin's
Autobiography (1771–1790, 1818) and *The Education of
Henry Adams* (1907, 1918). But there were scores of
others and also numerous variations on the basic form.
The seventeenth and eighteenth centuries, for example,

produced spiritual autobiographies and narratives of Indian captivity, while the nineteenth century continued
with the captivity narratives of black slaves. In the colonial period the old-world "conduct book," a parental guide
to children entering business and practical affairs, was
popular and probably influenced Franklin's decision to
cast his life story as a long letter to his son. Readers in
the eighteenth and nineteenth centuries also liked the
lurid confessions of notorious criminals, which they read
as moral examples of ill behavior and a bad end. Meanwhile, soldiers, sailors, frontiersmen, social workers and
businessmen wrote lives of adventure, discovery, and rises
from rags to riches. Such a range of forms and purposes
makes American autobiography, in a recent writer's
phrase, not a single genre but a "cluster of genres." [11]

Reading the *Autobiography*

Steffens borrowed from some of these special traditions of autobiography. A reading of his book can begin
with the way he used modes established by others.

It is enough to recall how important the birth of Pete
was to the origins of the *Autobiography* to see in it something of the conduct book. Showing Pete the difference
between political rhetoric and political reality seemed no
less practical than the older values of effective social dis-
course or making money. The *Autobiography* itself and
the letters he wrote about its messages have a sense of
urgency that a more casual reminiscence would not have
had.

Steffens's book borrows a little from the confessional
mode, too. Jean-Jacques Rousseau's *Confessions* (1781,
1788) established the form and remained the archetype
for an autobiography that excavated only the sinful and
despicable elements of one's behavior. The purpose was
not so much to titillate the reader with secret stories as
to challenge him to examine his own life and find a bet-

ter character. The ultimate effect of the challenge in Rousseau's *Confessions* was to establish the writer's *virtue,*
demonstrated by an extravagant humbling of himself.

Steffens's organizing principle is far different, but his
tendency toward self-accusation is nonetheless unmistakable. Much of it concerns sex and love. He realized, for
example, that the women he knew always loved him more
than he loved in return. From his mother and sisters, from
Mrs. Neely, a childless neighbor who lavished affection
on him as a boy, to his first wife, Josephine, Steffens
received more than he gave. The *Autobiography* makes a
conscious and extended show of his failing and of the
longing it left in others. One of Steffens's apologies for
his unloving nature is that, like many boys, he received
affection so early and freely that he never had to earn love
by giving it.[12]

But another explanation brings a further confession:
he remembered the day he learned about sex. At the age
of six, he built a treehouse, and one day a bigger boy
appeared:

He climbed up the tree, crept into my hut, looked it over, ap-
proving with his nodding head; then he looked at me. I
shrank from that look. I didn't know why, but there was something queer in it, something ugly, alarming. He reassured me,
and when I was quiet and fascinated, he began there in that
dark, tight, hidden little hut to tell me and show me sex. It
was perverse, impotent, exciting, dirty—it was horrible, and
when we sneaked into the nice, clean dust of the sunlit ground
I ran away home. I felt so dirty and ashamed that I wanted
to escape unseen to the bathroom, but my mother was in the
living-room I had to pass through, and she smiled and touched
me fondly. Horrid!

"Don't, oh, don't!" I cried, and I shrank away appalled.

"Why! What is the matter?" she asked, astonished and
hurt.

"I dunno," I said, and I ran upstairs. Locking the bathroom door, I answered no calls or knocks. I washed my hands,
my face, again and again till my father came home.[13]

Thereafter any sign of affection meant something dirty and fascinating, and the point would be reinforced some time later by "a certain servant girl" who taught him more and made him remember it. "Vividly," he says, "I can still see at times her hungry eyes, her panting, open mouth, and feel her creeping hands." The memory of those experiences with sex was not just vivid in its detail but almost inescapable in later years in the "lesson" it taught. Sex would be fascinating but dirty, and love of women would be refined and sexless. His friend Fred Howe wanted him to cut these paragraphs from the *Autobiography*, but Steffens argued for their place: "There are men who cannot love fully a refined woman (their wife, for example) and so seek out now and then some gross creature who represents to them what sex is to them; a rather dirty, loose thing of vice. I was started off in this direction by that first experience of mine which coupled dirt and disgust, a sort of horror of fascination, with my image or sense of love." Lottie, his sister, did not like the parts on sex either, and to her Steffens argued not the meaning of the confession, as he did to Fred and Marie Howe, but simply the merit of confessing "the weak or the wicked side" for its own sake.[14]

Steffens would have taken his self-accusation a step further if one woman in particular had allowed him. In his last year at Berkeley he was engaged, as noted earlier, to Gussie Burgess. Once he was in Germany, he became ambivalent about the relationship and broke their engagement with a careless but guilty ineptitude. Then he married Josephine and lived with her until she died in 1911. Soon after that he drifted back into love with Gussie again, and they carried on a prolonged affair until Steffens met Ella Winter and married her.

His uneasy relations with Gussie—using her and jilting her twice—made him feel guilty without making him reform. He would at least like to have shamed himself publicly in the *Autobiography*, but Gussie made him promise not to mention her by name or in disguise anywhere in the book. That was why writing about the 1890s and the 1910s was slow and depressing. He wanted to confess. "I promised, but it's too bad," he told Laura. "What I really am is shown by that story better than any other." [15]

Steffens's confessions about love and sex were probably sincere. But self-accusation is much more a pose in the chapter, "Muckraking Myself—A Little." The chapter is supposed to show how Steffens discovered that he was himself one of the "good men" he had been attacking as righteous hypocrites in his muckraking pieces. The discovery is built, characteristically, around two stories. In the first, Josephine accuses him of unwarranted idealism in believing his fellow muckrakers share his assumption that personal credit for an article matters less than publication for its own sake and the sake of reform. When she gets Ray Stannard Baker to give a selfish explanation of the origins of his famous "Capital and Labor Hunt Together" without mentioning Steffens, who gave him the article's whole thesis, Steffens sees she is right: "She won, smiled, and I felt—yellow; whether with jealousy of Baker or humiliation at the defeat of my wife, I don't know." [16]

The second story puts Steffens on a train a little later, alone in a big Pullman car except for an attentive and engaging black porter. He sends the porter away explaining that "I have to find and face my yellow streak and convince myself that I'm a crook." After a few hours' thought he realizes that more than anything else, he *was* jealous of Baker, which meant he put his personal interest above the general goal of reform. The porter returns. " 'Did ya catch the crook, boss?' he asked. 'No,' I said, 'I saw the yellow, and now I've got to see the crook.' " A few more hours bring the revelation that in a broader sense Steffens found himself holding back from writing the whole truth on a given subject or coloring a fact here and there "to keep my job, to keep my credit, to hold my readers and 'get by' my editors." In short, Steffens discovers he is a bribe-taker, a crook. "The porter that day, as he was brushing me off, said that I acted more's if I'd escaped than's if I'd got caught. 'I did,' I said, 'I caught myself and then I let myself go.' " [17]

The value of all this as confession is qualified by the fact that after twenty-five years the jealousy persisted. He was still mostly intent on showing that Baker's article was really his, as if to settle an old score. Beyond that, however, is the fact that by facing and admitting his own corruption, Steffens, like Rousseau, transforms himself into a virtuous man. He had often defined the terms: "good men" were righteous hypocrites; "bad men" were criminal but honest. So what Steffens confessed to in "Muckraking Myself—A Little" was, finally, *honesty*, the virtue of admitting evil. Now that he had caught himself, Steffens did indeed let himself go.

Whatever Steffens's *Autobiography* borrowed from earlier traditions, his book was especially responsive to a relatively new mode: the life as education. Thomas Cooley has recently distinguished between two broad forms in American autobiography: the "cultivated life" and the "educated life." [18] Telling one's story as a cultivated life, as Benjamin Franklin does, for example, assumes that character appears in embryo from early childhood and remains constant throughout the life and the story of the life. The autobiography shows the development and elaboration—the cultivation—of many innate capacities from first consciousness through middle age. The narrator's focus is always on the consistency of his being's inner principle.

The concept of the educated life was a late-nineteenth century form which assumed that the subject's character changed and adapted itself over time to external forces. In contrast to the cultivated life, the educated life involves a long process of learning, and the shape of one's life is not known until it is finished. *The Education of Henry Adams* is the classic example, but Lincoln Steffens's story is an educated life, too.[19]

Steffens's story consists of his early illusions, formal miseducation and long re-education. His dominant persona is that of an innocent, or, as he put it himself more precisely, "an innocent sufferer." [20] He does not so much shape the world as he is shaped by it, a world separate from him and willful. Gradually his naivete is stripped away so that by the 1920's, the decade in which Steffens wrote his autobiography, the boy has become a man and the man has become wise.

None of this was new. The unlearning theme was, for him, an old one: the dichotomy between innocence and knowledge had framed his journalism and fiction alike. There was a difference, of course, in that Steffens's earlier innocents opened their eyes quickly when circumstances thrust them into a confrontation with reality, whereas his own progress is irregular and lifelong. But continuity between his earlier characters and his autobiographical self is unmistakable. The logic that connects them can, perhaps, be drawn from Steffens himself, explaining at one point how he plumbed the character of one or another man he was to interview: ". . . when I wanted to get at the springs of thought and action in a man I was to write about, I should ask him about other men, and usually the witness would attribute to all others the motives and purposes which guided him." [21] Long before writing his *Autobiography*, Steffens saw himself as an innocent rudely educated, and, like the "witness" in his interviews, he freely imposed that persona on people he wrote about. Then in the *Autobiography* he re-embraced it formally himself.

Steffens presents his education as a series of stages which correspond generally to the large, titled sections into which the book is divided. In the first stage he is a Tom Sawyer character, wandering all over the American and Sacramento River valleys imagining he is, by turns, a Crusader, a trapper, a Comanche, an evangelist and Napoleon. These are harmless fantasies, but he has other "idealizations" which are not harmless and must be broken as his education begins. Men who are his father's friends and ought, therefore, to be trustworthy, for example, promise the boy things they cannot give. A horse race viewed from the grandstand appears honest, but the same race secretly arranged from the stable underneath is demonstrably crooked. Glib promises and fixed races suggest that a larger reality lies beneath what the boy-Steffens is expected to believe about the world.[22]

The first stage takes him through adolescence and assumes that his education is wholly unsought.[23] But the second stage, beginning with chapter fourteen, "All Through With Heroism," casts him as a conscious seeker after truth. "Imprisoned" for violating his preparatory school's drinking rule, Steffens receives a visit from his father and has to listen to an indictment of *himself* as a fraud. "All that worries me is your posings," the father says, "the bunk you have seemed always to like. I never saw you do anything for the sake of doing it; you always wanted to tell about it and see yourself and be seen doing it. That's poppycock. It does no harm in a boy, but you'll soon be no longer a boy, and there are a lot of men I know who are frauds and bunkers all their lives." [24] At the same time, Steffens calls for books and, as he reads, begins to question not just the "bunk" in himself but the validity of everything he has ever been taught. He is "all through with heroism" now not only for himself in, say, his Napoleon pose, but through more generally with the heroic in history and with any other unrealistic, untested idea.

Resolving not to leave his education any more to chance, Steffens sets out on a series of physical journeys which parallel and are a metaphor of his intellectual journey. He will eventually go from California to Europe, to urban America, to countries in the midst of revolution, and finally back to California again. For the moment, however, his education takes him only to the University of California at Berkeley, which teaches him more memorizable and useless bunk and, from there, to Germany, where Steffens, as autobiographer, reduces his life to a sharply schematic level. The European university chapters leave much of the early *Autobiography*'s charm and characterization behind as they chronicle Steffens's fruitless search for a reasonable ethics through Berlin, Heidelberg, Munich, Leipzig and Paris.

The section called "Seeing New York First" covers Steffens's life as a newspaperman in the 1890's, the third stage of his education. It also introduces a tension between Steffens's attempt to control his learning, on the one hand, and the willfulness of the world on the other, expressed often as uncontrollable fate. Thus, he returns to the United States intending to study American morals by entering business and politics, but fate, in the form of his father's unexpected withdrawal of support, stops him in New York where he must "hustle" for himself. He becomes a newspaperman but finds that as a reporter and later as a muckraker he does not actively discover the realities he seeks as much as they are revealed to him in apparently chance encounters.

Meanwhile, though he has been disillusioned many times already, Steffens's arrival in New York has the effect of reducing him to innocence again. He does not know even the rudiments of reporting, not even how to make up the "space bill" according to which reporters are paid. He is equally unprepared for the lessons he must learn. During the Lexow Committee's investigation of police corruption, for example, criminals and Committee supporters alike chide him for not seeing the vast system of municipal and social dishonesty beneath the petty crimes visible on the surface. "What do you do, read the papers or work for them?" a cynical reporter asks. Tammany boss Richard Croker, who calls him "boy," speaks more kindly but no less knowingly when he tells Steffens he ought to know better. "Would I never see through the appearance of things to the facts?" Steffens asks himself. "Never get past the lie to the truth?" [25]

Yet, by whatever chances he came to his Mulberry Street beat, Steffens is there and he learns. The clearest demonstration of that fact is his ability to match his grow-ing knowledge of political pay-offs, vice rings and kick-backs against the innocence of other greenhorns like The-odore Roosevelt. Arriving in New York as President of the Board of Police Commissioners in 1895, Steffens's Roosevelt is a political adolescent, a somewhat more vola-tile version of himself a few years before. He must be taught, and Steffens, with Jacob Riis, appoints himself teacher. That stance carries him through the remaining chapters of "Seeing New York First" and concludes the third stage of his education.

The fourth stage, "Muckraking," moves Steffens from New York to the national scene which has the effect of reducing him to innocence again, as though what he learned in New York did not prepare him for the national scope of corruption he would encounter after joining *Mc-Clure's Magazine* in 1901. Steffens's detailed evocation of the exhaustion which reduced him physically and men-tally in the summer of that year underscores the regres-sion he experiences as he goes from "Seeing New York First" to "Muckraking."

His life as a muckraker begins, appropriately, more with accidents than intentions. Steffens describes it so him-self when he says:

. . . my contribution to history would be, not a letter, not a philosophical dissertation, but a story, a confession of inno-cence. I did not intend to be a muckraker; I did not know that I was one till President Roosevelt picked the name out of Bunyan's *Pilgrim's Progress* and pinned it on us; and even then he said he did not mean me. Those were innocent days; we were all innocent folk; but no doubt all movements, whether for good or for evil, are as innocent of intention as ours.[26]

Accordingly, Steffens stresses the chances by which S. S. McClure sent him on a tour of American cities and by which he met Joseph Folk, Hovey Clarke, and a whole succession of surprised, embattled municipal reformers. Then, gradually, the corruption in one city after the other appears less a coincidence and more a pattern, so that Steffens, a *naïf* who thought, with all Americans, that bad government came from bad politicians, learns that bad government comes instead from businessmen, whose interests benefit—even require—the corruption of city councils, state legislatures and the national government. All this means Steffens is learning again, and, as usual, his teachers are the wise political bosses themselves: the bad men who are good. One of them, Iz Durham of Philadelphia, confirms his progress by telling him, using an image Steffens obviously likes, "Oh, I can see that you are a born crook that's gone straight." [27]

By 1908, having written *The Shame of the Cities* and *The Struggle for Self-Government,* he knows enough to want to stop muckraking and, in rejecting it, to define muckraking for the first time, too. "I had come so definitely to the conclusion," he said, "that man's ideas were determined by the teachings of his childhood, by his business interests, by his environment, and not by logic, that muckraking looked useless. Society moved like a glacier, slowly; if it progressed, it grew like an oak tree—slowly. One might water and manure the soil about it, but it was no use shouting at it." [28] Muckraking assumed that government corruption was merely willful, both on the part of the businessmen and their politicians and also the public which tolerated them. As a muckraker, Steffens had exhorted his readers to eliminate corruption by an equally powerful exercise of will. Now, in 1908, he could see that the origins of social behavior were older and its

movement more natural—glacial, oaklike—than he had
known.

That called for a change in approach, and the change
introduces the next section, "Revolution," which is also
the fifth stage of Steffens's education: "Nothing but revolution could change the system, I thought." Using a
logic and will he had just finished denying to man in
general, Steffens decides in 1909 to move for a time
among "the revolutionists: the reds, the socialists, anar-
chists, the I.W.W.'s, and the single-taxers, who all seemed
to seek the roots of the matter." [29] Clearly, Steffens has
encountered a major change in his life, and, in the section on "Revolution," which covers the years from 1909
to 1927, he merges two decades of world upheaval with
upheavals in his own thinking as he experiences the Mc-
Namara bombing, the outbreak of world war, the Mexican Revolution, the Russian Revolution, and the advent of
fascism.

His persona changes, too. He has not wholly lost his
innocence, since he is still willing to sit like a slow pupil
before, say, V. I. Lenin, as the great, wise, angry dictator
delivers eloquent answers to Steffens's naive questions.
Lenin is another tough, honest boss, and so, near the end
of "Revolution," is Benito Mussolini.[30] But chance no
longer shapes his life and, more often than before, Steffens himself plays the role of mentor. In the chapter
called "Settling the Dynamiters' Case," for example, he
wins General Harrison Gray Otis, whose newspaper, the
Los Angeles Times, was the target of an anarchist bomb,
over to labor's point of view. Otis agrees to compromise
on the McNamara case after listening to a five-minute
speech from a very tough, knowledgeable Steffens. Later
he confronts Elbert H. Gary, President of the United
States Steel Corporation, and convinces him that his "wel-
fare work" among his labor force earns him only the
workers' resentment because he grants them just what *he*
thinks is good for them. The explanation takes only a

few minutes and is only occasionally interrupted by Gary's thoughtful and convinced, "So that's it, is it?" [31]

"Seeing America at Last" is the last stage and is described in the shortest space. Steffens returns to California from his expatriation and, at the age of sixty-one, can finally see America in the context of an inexorably evolving world civilization. Its goal is total rationalization and democratization, and its media of change are business efficiency and red revolution alike. It was wrong, he now sees, to despise businessmen and politicians, each of whose behavior as well as the nexus between them was inevitable and ultimately good.

That he had to unlearn all the "taught ignorance" of his day and educate himself through experience leaves him nonetheless optimistic. "My spiral-like story ends as it began:" he writes on the *Autobiography*'s last page, recalling an image from its first, "by my being thrown out of bed by the shocks of an earthquake which laid me out, not crying, however, but smiling. My life was worth my living. And as for the world in general, all that was or is or ever will be wrong with that is my—our thinking about it." [32] In other words, the world simply and inevitably exists, and we may learn and be taught about it well or badly, correctly or incorrectly, the space between these two options defining the world's seeming but unreal disorder.

Steffens is an unusually successful autobiographer because his book satisfies, often brilliantly, all the requirements of the genre. The *craft* of autobiography is, after all, at least as important as the life itself. Steffens's sensitivity to the historical development of his life is obvious: his account is no self-portrait drawn at a single moment. Indeed, he writes less about being than about becoming. And he is careful to evoke himself in meaningful relation to the rest of the world, which is not just a setting painted, as it were, behind Steffens's growing character, but is instead an active participant in his very education.

The fact that Steffens casts much of the *Autobiography* in the form of dialogues—extended conversations with bosses, reformers, children, revolutionaries, and presidents—builds the essential connection between himself and the world into the very strategy of his narration.

The *Autobiography* is also closely organized around a philosophy of life, which, in Steffens's case, meant not just that society was evolving toward a happy outcome (whether it be communism or some other form of social rationalization), but that on the level of day-to-day living, the world was reducible to two categories: first appearances and final realities. Steffens's *Autobiography* showed, in other words, that life was almost never what it seemed. This theme was obviously appropriate to the construction of his own life as an education, but Steffens extended the dichotomy between appearance and reality to so many other lives as well that it becomes the matrix governing everyone's experience. This breadth of application suggests that the dichotomy had become the commonest assumption in Steffens's thinking.

So much in the *Autobiography* turns on the matching of appearances and reality that a few examples only highlight what is a pervasive principle. Probably the classic demonstration that there *is* a difference, however, is the chapter called "I Make a Crime Wave" in which Steffens tells how in the 1890's he and Jacob Riis fought a friendly war by having their rival papers publish police crime reports that were normally too common to be published anywhere. For a few weeks, Steffens says, readers of the *Post* and *Sun* had the false impression of an upsurge in crime. When Theodore Roosevelt, President of the Police Board, privately ordered them to stop, the "crime wave" passed, and the unknowing public falsely credited Roosevelt with effective police work in ending it.[33]

The crime wave was an innocent joke. Steffens takes misrepresentation more seriously in two other kinds of experience. One is *bluffing*, frequently an instrument in his

own education, and the other is *fantasy*, a pathetic, sometimes willful avoidance of reality.

Steffens's bluffing is conscious and, in the *Autobiography*, self-confessed. As a young reporter, much aware
of how little he knows, he frequently pretends to know
more than he does during interviews, hoping to draw
his subject into extended revelations. Or, as in the case
of a meeting with J. P. Morgan, arbiter of Wall Street
finance, he defies his subject with a tough assault. Morgan's impenetrability was legendary, but Steffens must
beard the lion in his den to make him interpret a press
release on the bond market:

"Mr. Morgan," I said as brave as I was afraid, "What does
this statement mean?" and I threw the paper down before
him.

"Mean!" he exclaimed. His eyes glared, his great red
nose seemed to me to flash and darken, flash and darken.
Then he roared. "Mean! It means what it says. I wrote it myself, and it says what I mean."

"It doesn't say anything—straight," I blazed.

He sat back there, flashing and rumbling; then he
clutched the arms of his chair, and I thought he was going
to leap at me. I was so scared that I defied him.

"Oh, come now, Mr. Morgan," I said, "you may know a
lot about figures and finance, but I'm a reporter, and I know
as much as you do about English. And that statement isn't
English."

That was the way to treat him, I was told afterward.
And it was in that case. He glared at me a moment more, the
fire went out of his face, and he leaned forward over the bit
of paper and said very meekly, "What's the matter with it?" [34]

Morgan sits while Steffens rewrites the statement under his eyes and then as the reporter leaves, mutters,
"Knows what he wants, and—and—gets it." Morgan's
judgment confirms both Steffens's ignorance and his
growing awareness. He does not know much, but at least
his bluff shows he understands what he ought to know.
Morgan is hardly an innocent, but Steffens's appearance

momentarily has him fooled. Much later, during Steffens's muckraking tour of American cities and states, he finds that his reputation as an expert on corruption, however undeserved, precedes him and allows a nearly effortless continuation of his bluff. "Oh, hell," says an attorney for some Missouri boodlers who meets him for the first time, "I thought you were six feet tall." [35]

Sometimes, though, Steffens's bluff goes in the other direction: he pretends innocence. Often he seems to swallow fairy tales from police and politicians in order to trick them into being more careless in their talk or to shock them, when he turns around, with a sudden display of knowledge. He tells a story of Wisconsin's anti-LaFollette "stalwarts," for example, who invited him to lunch and matched him against a clever lawyer who, with seeming success, fills Steffens with silly lies about their political deals. Then Steffens explains the same events according to his own truer investigation and dramatically wins the day. "The incident," he wrote, "told and retold, helped me greatly: it discouraged lying to me and spread the impression that I knew what I pretended to inquire about. . . ." [36]

If bluff is a controlled management of appearance and reality, fantasy represents appearance and reality out of control. There is nothing wrong, of course, with Steffens's boyhood fantasies; indeed, they are as charming as anything in the *Autobiography*. But persistent allegiance to imaginative and impossible dreams can only mean being controlled by them. Some characters, then, are pathetic: Mrs. Neely, who tries to transfer her own failed dream of being a minister to Steffens as a boy; Duke, the son of an English lord who tries unhappily to fulfill his fantasy of cowboy life; and the American psychology student in Leipzig ("afterward one of the leading men in American science and education") who, out of loyalty to the master, Wilhelm Wundt, falsifies his experimental results to bring them into accord with revered theory.[37] Such characters model the danger Steffens must escape.

Since craft and design determine the success of an autobiography, something further should be said of Steffens's craftsmanship and narrative strategy.

Early in its composition, Steffens indicated that he knew what his autobiography's format, apart from the staged progress toward wisdom, must be. "It is not muckraking, philosophy or even fact knowledge," he wrote to a friend. "I think it is an understanding story which anybody can read and like and join in on. Indeed so far, it is a series of short stories. . . ." [38] From beginning to end, the *Autobiography* remains a series of loosely connected stories, most of which can be read separately. As long as one or another chapter makes Steffens himself its central character, or, at least the character in whose presence and for whose benefit others develop, the book's loose structure is successful and does not needlessly fragment Steffens's life. He is at his best when characters met in one chapter reappear later either in fact or in, for example, the boy-Steffens's memory. Thus at one point Mr. Neely reminisces sadly for Steffens's hearing about the false tales of the "golden west" which drew him and Mrs. Neely to California, and the boy sees that the expression on Neely's face at that moment is like Duke the cowboy's and other fantasizers he has met.[39] The loose structure gets out of hand, however, in a few of the chapters that detail Steffens's muckraking exploits. "Ben Lindsey: the Kids' Judge," for example, explains the philosophy of the famous juvenile court judge without any special relation to Steffens's development. The chapter lacks the usual dialogue between Steffens and his characters which might have developed the autobiographical need for Lindsey's inclusion. Yet, even when such dialogues appear in chapters like "Timber Frauds in Oregon" or "A Successful

Failure" (about Steffens's friend E. A. Filene), the chapters are flat and seem to degenerate from autobiography to mere reminiscence of men and events.

What the story format allows him to do, often very well, is to *demonstrate* the points he wants to make rather than merely assert them. Chapter VI, "A Painter and a Page," for example, is a nicely unified tale which makes use of images normally thought to be disharmonious in order to establish a lesson Steffens had to learn early: that "nothing was what it was supposed to be." He meets W. M. Marple, a landscape painter who shows the boy that an artist paints not the land itself but what he "sees," what he perceives. Then Marple introduces him to his son, Charlie, who takes Steffens to the state legislature where Charlie Marple has an appointment as a page. Charlie shows him that the official business on the floor of the assembly is a "front" and does not correspond to the actual government carried on in Sacramento hotel rooms. The chapter develops the appearance-reality dichotomy, to be sure, but it does something else as well. Steffens's ironic juxtaposition of art and politics demonstrates the crudeness and lack of differentiation in his youthful thinking. Art *would* seem a "front" for reality only to a boy who is thinking his way through life for the first time. Later Steffens would learn to respect the legitimacy and "reality" of art. For the moment, however, the subject of "A Painter and a Page" can only be the too-simple manner in which Steffens *first* began to understand the difference between reality and construction of reality.

Another story, "Munich: There Are No Artists," makes the point, through an extended demonstration, that the European universities he toured as a student could offer nothing more serious and worthwhile in art than they could in ethics. Having exhausted the resources of Heidelberg, Steffens goes to Munich and accepts an American art student, Carlos Hittel, as his guide. Hittel fills his ears with withering criticism of other Munich artists. Then, when Steffens and a group of art students visit Venice, Hittel himself is unmasked. Steffens tells it as a story: as they are about to leave Venice, Hittel suggests they walk from their hotel to the railway station. The others protest they will lose their way in the city's labyrinth of streets, but Hittel says that anyone, especially a Westerner like himself with a good sense of direction, can find his way. Some, including Steffens, go with Hittel, the others take some public conveyance. Hittel, "swift as an Indian" (to the amazement of all) arrives at the station an hour ahead of time. Only later does he tell Steffens that Venetian intersections are marked with a sign, "Alla Strada Ferrata"—"To the Railway." [40]

Steffens had used the railway station story before, in a sketch for the *New York Commercial Advertiser* as early as 1899.[41] Then it was a charming tale but no more than that. In his autobiography he tells it as an extended metaphor of fraud. Impressed with Hittel's art and his plainsman's sense of direction, Steffens praises him to the other art students. They respond with a withering, and to Steffens, a disillusioning indictment of Hittel's art. "Never works," they say, "only talks art, drinks, brags, and runs down everybody else." The indictment makes sense, however, only because it has been set up by the more detailed telling of the "Alla Strada Ferrata" story. Indeed, since Steffens does not offer any substantive critique of Hittel's or anyone else's art, the railway station tale largely replaces substance with metaphor, demonstrating a point and skirting it at the same time.

The presence of Steffens's literary craft suggests an important question: how accurate is the *Autobiography*? How faithful an account of his life is it? Dialogue makes up a large part of the book, and one wonders, for example, how he could remember the substance and language of so many conversations, even the exact German of the university chapters and, later, speeches from Lenin, even though he admits he did not know Russian and had

to rely on interpreters. A friend who read these conversations asked Steffens how it was, in any case, that "*you*
always come out on top." Steffens's tongue-in-cheek reply—"Well, damn it, I'm a reporter. *I* always did."—
recognized, at least, that the doubt was legitimate.[42]

Further, Steffens seems to have changed the characters of some people he met to suit his autobiographical
needs. Richard Croker, the leader of Tammany Hall at
the turn of the century, appears in the *Autobiography* as
a gentle, fatherly teacher who tries to show a surprised
Steffens the business connection to everything around
him. James B. Dill, architect of the New Jersey trust laws,
has a similar character: open-minded and patient as he
explains the world to his naive pupil, whom he calls "Dr.
Innocent." Yet Steffens's original writing on Croker and
Dill decades earlier was somewhat less sympathetic and
his own personal relationship to them more worldly.[43]

On the other hand, one should not automatically as-
sume that Steffens's *Autobiography* is a book of lies and
distortions. The opportunity to compare Steffens's memory of a conversation with an account by the other party
is rare, but it is worth noting that Steffens's account of
his first meeting with Martin Lomasney, boss of Boston
politics, is not much different from Lomasney's own version set down in notes made immediately afterward. Both
remembered that Lomasney's opening was blunt and that
Steffens was at first intimidated by the "Boston Mahatma."
Once they established mutual respect, however, their relationship grew to the point where Steffens could intercede
with Lomasney on behalf of Boston reformers.[44]

The question of accuracy in Steffens's or anyone else's
autobiography is only relevant depending upon one's use
of the account. A biographer or historian of Steffens's
time would examine the differences between truth and distortion carefully. He would know, in any case, that he
could not rely on the *Autobiography* as his only source.
But the critic of the *Autobiography* as a work of art,

a contribution to a genre with its own potentialities and limitations looks for the very creativity and imagination which in a strictly historical reading would be seen as distortion and exaggeration. Autobiographies can, of course, be closer or farther from the truth, but it is worth saying again that writing *any* autobiography is by definition a creative and, therefore, distorting act.

Whatever compromises Steffens made between design and truth, he did try hard to recapture his mental state at one time or another in his life. And he tried to write about events no further ahead in his understanding of them than he understood at the time he experienced them. Keeping later conclusions in suspension seemed easy when he was writing about the boy's discovering point of view, what he called "the merely wandering mentality of that age," but he knew it would be harder to narrate his experiences with more public events—"things all men know"—as a series of revelations.[45] Once when Marie Howe, his editor, cautioned about the egotism in his characterization of Theodore Roosevelt as President of the New York Board of Police Commissioners, Steffens explained that he was trying to say something about himself in the 1890s as much as about Roosevelt:

I had respect for [Jacob] Riis; he knew something about the police; I had awe of Max, Riis' boy; he understood everything. But Roosevelt? He knew nothing and I could not see how he was ever going to be taught all that I had to teach him.

What is more, I think he also felt his ignorance and wished he knew as much as Riis and I did. This all amused me as I wrote it. Remembering my conceit, I wrote passages in the exact state of mind of that period; I was the superior, "wise" police reporter again, and my mistake was that I thought readers, like you, would laugh and enjoy it too.[46]

Because he wrote about men and events but also about his step-by-step experience of them, Steffens's *Autobiography* has a sense of mild suspense, which a book composed as a series of foregone conclusions would not have.

Perhaps the best example of Steffens's withholding information from the reader until he "knows" it himself involves the tale of his German university friend, Johann Friedrich Krudewolf, a story which is among the most sensitive in the whole *Autobiography*.[47] One meets Krudewolf as Steffens did, on an art history outing near Heidelberg: ". . . a tall young German came up to me, struck his heels together, saluted stiffly, and said: 'My name is Johann Friedrich Krudewolf. I am German; I take you for an American. I want to learn English. I propose to exchange with you lessons in German for lessons in English." Steffens accepts and soon they become good friends, but the formality of the opening sets the tone for their relationship as Steffens—not Krudewolf— came to accept it. They travel together, spend weeks in each other's company, but, though Steffens offers a few hints that their friendship had deep, if unexpressed, meaning for Krudewolf, he is much less involved himself and casts their relationship wholly in terms of their excursions through various river valleys. Steffens is surprised, then, and a little annoyed, when, just as he is about to leave for America, Krudewolf summons him to a sanitarium and asks him about scholarships in American universities, and about Steffens's father and mother, and finally whether "if anything happened to him, I might return to Germany and do something he might want done." Steffens is reluctant but gives his promise.

The *Autobiography* explains these things as incidental to Steffens's other European activities because, whatever meaning they take on later, they *were* incidental to other experiences. He delays the full explanation of the Krudewolf mystery more than a hundred pages until Krudewolf's death in 1895 when Steffens himself learned for the first time the significant details of his friend's life that cast his earlier scant knowledge in a new light.

What he discovers in 1895 is that Krudewolf had made him chief heir to his considerable estate. The story of Steffens's return to Germany multiplies into three interconnected stories which together explain Krudewolf's behavior and comment on Steffens's own. The first is Steffens's trip itself to Lehe near Bremen to settle Krudewolf's affairs. In the midst of his own career, he resents having to go at all, but this feeling is matched by shame that he seldom had answered Krudewolf's letters promptly and that their relationship had centered mostly on his, not Krudewolf's doings. The tone of confession is strong.

The second story deals with Krudewolf's meticulous attorney, W. Lorenz, who handles the details of the estate and who interprets to Steffens some important Krudewolf family history. But Steffens takes time to evoke Lorenz himself: another fantasizer who, in his mind, travels extensively, calculating the last details of time and expense without ever leaving his dining room table and a veritable library of Baedecker travel guides. Steffens looks at him one night, "the look not of man to man, but of kid to kid," and recalls his own life as a trapper or explorer and thinks, too, of the grown-ups who dreamed too long into adulthood that they were something other than what they really were.

The third story, of course, takes up Krudewolf himself. In some ways, it is reminiscent of Thomas Mann (or, considering that Steffens wrote an earlier version in a letter of 1895, perhaps it anticipates Mann [48]) in its contrast between art and business, northern and southern Europe and its pairing of youth and death. In the attic of the family home, Steffens finds a basket containing two bridal wreaths, some jewelry, an account book, and two return tickets to Bremen. He realizes that Krudewolf himself arranged the articles together as symbols of his and his family's life, and discussions with relatives confirm their significance. Krudewolf was the son of a businessman who expected Johann to enter and continue the fam-

ily business, built up, as the account book shows, over
generations of time. But the son's artistic temperament,
supported by his mother and stepmother and symbolized
by the floral wreaths Johann saved, brought him into conflict with his father. He longed to escape, and so did his
stepmother, who did not live to use the tickets—only to
Bremen, a commercial city—which her partly repentant
husband brought her on her deathbed. When the father
died, Johann did escape, to the universities and art history, only to be pursued by relatives angered by his rejection of the family calling.

Steffens learns, too, that when he died, Krudewolf
bequeathed virtually everything to him because he pro-
jected his own predicament as a conflict experienced by
the world in general. And he believed that Steffens's uneasy relationship with his father recapitulated his own.
The money would free Steffens as he himself had never
been free.

The story is told as well as any in the *Autobiography*,
and it also recalls and highlights some themes which Steffens exhibits elsewhere: his tendency toward self-accusation, his being loved more than he loves in return, his
ambiguous relations with his father, his own uneasy stance
between art and materialism, and, of course, his vision of
essential truths revealed as discreet, quasi-fictive stories.

In any case, the Krudewolf story shows what all of his
work shows: that Steffens was as much a *writer* as he was
a reporter. If the *Autobiography* was, as autobiography
must be, an imaginative arrangement of events in a man's
personal history, it is no less true that everything else he
wrote drew upon the same imagination.

What he wrote for the *New York Post* and the *Commercial Advertiser* were not neutral descriptions of reality; they were stories with an author-imposed integrity
and form. Much the same can be said of Steffens's muckraking. *The Shame of the Cities* was arresting not because
it called attention to government corruption but because

of the *way* it revealed corruption. Steffens's selection and characterization of men and events was as compelling as the substance of his work. When, in the revolutionary decade of the 1910s, he found himself searching for a new form to express the hope he saw in upheavals abroad, his search, though unsuccessful, confirmed the high place style held in his mind.

The theme that unites much of Steffens's writing is his sense of the distance between innocence and knowledge. The *Autobiography* offers the fullest expression of the dichotomy, but it had been near the center of his thinking from university days onward. Steffens is, in whichever story one encounters him, a discoverer, and so, again and again, are his characters. And what the last story—the *Autobiography*—does, finally, is to sum up not the experience of a single man but, in his view, the discoveries of a whole generation.

Notes

1. STUDENT AND TEACHER

1. Ella Winter and Granville Hicks, eds., *The Letters of Lincoln Steffens*, 2 vols. (New York: Harcourt, Brace, 1938), 1:375.
2. [E. L. Godkin], "Our Great Cities," *Nation*, 9 (Nov. 11, 1869):404.
3. Lincoln Steffens, *The Autobiography of Lincoln Steffens*, 2 vols. in 1 (New York: Harcourt, Brace, 1931), p. 385.
4. Winter and Hicks, *Letters of Lincoln Steffens*, 1:440.
5. Steffens, *Autobiography*, p. 77.
6. Ibid., p. 23.
7. Justin Kaplan, *Lincoln Steffens, A Biography* (New York: Simon and Schuster, 1974), p. 19.
8. Winter and Hicks, *Letters of Lincoln Steffens*, 1:7.
9. Ibid., 1:394.
10. Ibid., 1:11–12, 27, 40.
11. Ibid., 1:55.
12. Ibid., 1:62–3, 66–7.
13. Ibid., 1:67, 113–14.
14. Ibid., 1:45.
15. Ibid., 1:27–8.
16. Ibid., 1:79.
17. Fischer's work was *System der Logik und Metaphysik, oder Wissenschaftslehre* which appeared in 1852 and, in a second edition, 1865.
18. Winter and Hicks, *Letters of Lincoln Steffens*, 1:6–7, 13, 44, 68.

19. Ibid., 1:51.
20. Steffens, *Autobiography,* p. 169.

2. THE REPORTER

1. Quoted in Larzer Ziff, *The American 1890's, Life and Times of a Lost Generation* (New York: Viking, 1966), p. 150.
2. Winter and Hicks, *Letters of Lincoln Steffens,* 1:92. Ziff, *American 1890's,* p. 150.
3. Winter and Hicks, *Letters of Lincoln Steffens,* 1:91. Steffens, *Autobiography,* p. 170.
4. J. Lincoln Steffens, "Sweet Punch: A Monologue," *Harper's,* 88 (December 1893):127.
5. Winter and Hicks, *Letters of Lincoln Steffens,* 1:87. See also 1:90–1.
6. Allan Nevins, The Evening Post, *A Century of Journalism* (New York: Boni and Liveright, 1922) is the standard history.
7. Ibid., p. 530; Steffens, *Autobiography,* p. 179.
8. Steffens, *Autobiography,* pp. 184–85.
9. Nevins, Evening Post, pp. 529–30, 551–52.
10. Helen McGill Hughes, *News and the Human Interest Story* (Chicago: University of Chicago Press, 1940) is a useful introduction, though this field needs further investigation. George Juergens, *Joseph Pulitzer and the New York World* (Princeton: Princeton University Press, 1966) is useful; see also Robert Darnton, "Writing News and Telling Stories," *Daedalus,* 104 (Spring 1975):175–94.
11. "A Frenzied Italian," *New York Evening Post,* 24 October 1896, Lincoln Steffens Papers, Scrapbook 1, Columbia University Libraries. Steffens's spelling of names and foreign words has been preserved.
12. "J. J. Martin's Irritability," ibid., 18 October 1894.
13. "Italian Tailors Crossing the Bowery," ibid., 12 August 1896.
14. "New York Shop Girls," ibid., 2 July 1896.
15. "A Small Babel at a Fire," ibid., 1895 or 1896 (date uncertain).

16. "A Bird Dealer's Loss," ibid., July 1896. See also "Dying Groans Unheeded," ibid., c. September 1896 and Steffens, *Autobiography*, pp. 241–42 for similar evocations of this theme.

17. "Race War in Harlem," ibid., 18 July 1896.

18. J. Lincoln Steffens, "Bloke Murray's Golden Moon," *New York Commercial Advertiser*, 19 December 1897, Steffens Papers, Scrapbook 1.

19. J. L. Steffens, "Schloma, Daughter of Schmuhl," *Chap-Book*, 5 (June 15, 1896):128–32; Winter and Hicks, *Letters of Lincoln Steffens*, 1:123.

20. Jacob Riis, *How the Other Half Lives* (New York: Scribner's Sons, 1890), chs. 10 and 11; Steffens, *Autobiography*, p. 244.

21. Roy L. M'Cardell, "Notes Among the Newspapers," clipping, 1897, Steffens Papers, Scrapbook 1.

22. Winter and Hicks, *Letters of Lincoln Steffens*, 1:130; Steffens, *Autobiography*, pp. 313–19.

23. Winter and Hicks, *Letters of Lincoln Steffens*, 1:128–29; Steffens, *Autobiography*, p. 321.

24. Several of these, under various sub-headlines, are in Steffens Papers, Scrapbook 1.

25. "Heidelberg in Summer," *New York Commercial Advertiser*, 3 September 1898, Steffens Papers, Scrapbook 1; "The Painters Who Fail," ibid., 16 November 1898; "A Christmas Conquest," ibid., 24 December 1898; "An Unhappy Fishball," ibid., 24 December 1898; "Hide and Seek Mounted," ibid., 31 December 1898; "The Count and the Arch," ibid., 4 February 1899; "Alla Strada Ferrata," ibid., 11 February 1899. Steffens's interesting re-use of the material in the last article is discussed below, pp. 140–41.

26. Hutchins Hapgood, *Types from City Streets* (New York: Funk and Wagnalls, 1910), pp. 107–12; Winter and Hicks, *Letters of Lincoln Steffens*, 1:138.

3. MUCKRAKER

1. George Broadhurst, *The Man of the Hour* (New York: J. S. Ogilvie, 1906); Maxwell Bloomfield, "Muckraking

and the American Stage: The Emergence of Realism, 1905–1917," *South Atlantic Quarterly*, 66 (Spring 1967):165–178.

2. John E. Semonche, "Theodore Roosevelt's 'Muck-rake Speech': A Reassessment," *Mid-America*, 46 (April 1964):114–25.

3. Robert Stinson, "S. S. McClure and His Magazine: A Study in the Editing of *McClure's*, 1893–1913" (Ph.D. dissertation, Indiana University, 1971), pp. 160–86.

4. Steffens, *Autobiography*, p. 364. See also Winter and Hicks, *Letters of Lincoln Steffens*, 1:154–5.

5. Ida M. Tarbell, *All in the Day's Work, An Autobiography* (New York: Scribner's Sons, 1939), pp. 200–201.

6. J. Lincoln Steffens, "Great Types of Modern Business, VI.—Politics," *Ainslee's*, 8 (October 1901):213. Cf. Lincoln Steffens, *The Shame of the Cities* (New York: McClure, Phillips & Co., 1904; reprint ed., New York: Hill and Wang, 1957), p. 4.

7. Steffens, *Shame of the Cities*, p. 3.

8. Ibid., p. 9; Steffens, *Autobiography*, pp. 39–40.

9. Steffens, *Shame of the Cities*, pp. 98, 99.

10. Ibid., p. 171.

11. Steffens, *Autobiography*, p. 392.

12. Steffens, *Shame of the Cities*, pp. 138, 143.

13. Steffens, *Autobiography*, p. 401.

14. Steffens, *Shame of the Cities*, p. 106.

15. Ibid., pp. 19, 32, 58.

16. Ibid., pp. 44, 45–46.

17. Ibid., p. 12.

18. Winter and Hicks, *Letters of Lincoln Steffens*, 1:168.

19. Ibid., 1:162, 164, 165, 166.

20. Lincoln Steffens, *The Struggle for Self-Government* (New York: McClure, Phillips & Co., 1906; reprint ed., New York: Johnson Reprint Corporation, 1968), p. 42.

21. Ibid., pp. 4–5.

22. Winter and Hicks, *Letters of Lincoln Steffens*, 1:171.

23. Steffens, *Struggle for Self-Government*, p. 115.

24. Ibid., p. 3.

25. Steffens, *Autobiography*, p. 448.

26. Steffens, *Struggle for Self-Government*, pp. 12–13.

27. Ibid., pp. 211, 266, 284.
28. Ibid., p. 35.
29. Ibid., pp. 179–80.
30. Ibid., pp. 57–8.
31. Ibid., pp. 162, 163, 164, 172, 190.
32. Ibid., p. 173.
33. Ibid., pp. 177–8.
34. Ibid., p. 10.
35. "A Servant of God and the People," [Mark Fagan], *McClure's*, 26 (January 1907), 297–308; "The Gentleman from Essex" [Everett Colby], ibid. (February 1906):420–33; "Ben B. Lindsey: The Just Judge," ibid. 27 (October 1906):563–82, 28 (November, December 1906):74–88, 162–76; "Rudolph Spreckels," *American* 65 (February 1908):390–402; "U'Ren, The Law Giver," ibid. (March 1908), 527–40.
36. Lincoln Steffens, *Upbuilders* (New York: Doubleday, Page and Company, 1909; reprint ed., Seattle, Wash.: University of Washington Press, 1968), pp. 43, 152, 288. Steffens once thought to call the book *New Style Christians*. See Winter and Hicks, *Letters of Lincoln Steffens*, 1:212.
37. Lincoln Steffens, "The Least of These," *Everybody's*, 20 (January 1909):57–62.
38. Winter and Hicks, *Letters of Lincoln Steffens*, 1:223.
39. Lincoln Steffens, "Hearst, The Man of Mystery," *American*, 63 (November 1906):3–22; "Eugene V. Debs," *Everybody's*, 19 (October 1908):455–69.
40. Winter and Hicks, *Letters of Lincoln Steffens*, 2:1054 gives citations for the articles as they appeared in the *New York World*.

4. MEDIATOR

1. Kaplan, *Lincoln Steffens*, pp. 186–93.
2. Winter and Hicks, *Letters of Lincoln Steffens*, 1:336–7; Steffens, *Autobiography*, pp. 637–38.
3. Winter and Hicks, *Letters of Lincoln Steffens*, 1:383.
4. Ibid., 1:355.

5. Ibid., 1:348.

6. Lincoln Steffens, "The Sunny Side of Mexico," *Metropolitan*, 42 (May 1915):27–29, 55–56, reprinted in Ella Winter and Herbert Shapiro, eds., *The World of Lincoln Steffens* (New York: Hill and Wang, 1962), pp. 4–20.

7. Lincoln Steffens, "Bunk, A Story of Revolutionary Mexico," *Everybody's*, 36 (February 1917):200–211.

8. Lincoln Steffens, "The Great Lost Moment," *Everybody's*, 36 (March 1917):350–61.

9. Lincoln Steffens, "Making Friends With Mexico," *Collier's*, 58 (25 November 1916):5–6, reprinted in Winter and Shapiro, *World of Lincoln Steffens*, pp. 20–31; "Into Mexico and—Out!" *Everybody's*, 34 (May 1916):533–47.

10. Robert Freeman Smith, *The United States and Revolutionary Nationalism in Mexico, 1916–1932* (Chicago: University of Chicago Press, 1972), chs. 3 and 4, has a detailed interpretation of the war scare.

11. Winter and Shapiro, *World of Lincoln Steffens*, p. 2; Winter and Hicks, *Letters of Lincoln Steffens*, 1:368, 370.

12. Steffens, *Autobiography*, p. 737.

13. Ibid., p. 739.

14. Smith, *United States and Revolutionary Nationalism in Mexico*, pp. 51–62.

15. Lincoln Steffens, "Thirty-Threed, A Tale of Our Border Today," *Everybody's*, 35 (July 1916):41–51; Winter and Hicks, *Letters of Lincoln Steffens*, 1:376.

16. Winter and Hicks, *Letters of Lincoln Steffens*, 1:381.

17. Kaplan, *Lincoln Steffens*, pp. 233–34 says the Bolshevik Revolution brought on a psychological crisis for Steffens.

18. John M. Thompson, *Russia, Bolshevism, and the Versailles Peace* (Princeton: Princeton University Press, 1966), p. 162n.

19. Lincoln Steffens, "Rasputin—The Real Story," *Everybody's*, 37 (September 1917):276–85; "The Killing of Rasputin," *Everybody's*, 37 (October 1917):385–94.

20. Lincoln Steffens, "Midnight in Russia," *McClure's*, 50 (May 1918):22–24, 60, reprinted in Winter and Shapiro, *World of Lincoln Steffens*, pp. 34–51.

21. Christian, "The Rumor in Russia," *Nation*, 107 (21 December 1917) :766–67.
22. Kaplan, *Lincoln Steffens*, p. 243.
23. Thompson, *Russia, Bolshevism, and the Versailles Peace*, pp. 146–76, 246–67 is a detailed account of the Bullitt Mission.
24. Ibid., p. 175–76.
25. The Report is reprinted in Winter and Shapiro, *World of Lincoln Steffens*, pp. 55–66.
26. Lincoln Steffens, *Moses in Red* (originally published in Philadelphia: Dorrance, 1926), reprinted in Winter and Shapiro, *World of Lincoln Steffens*, p. 86.
27. Winter and Hicks, 1:462.
28. Ibid., 2:776.
29. Steffens, *Moses in Red* in Winter and Shapiro, *World of Lincoln Steffens*, p. 77.
30. Ibid., p. 75.
31. Winter and Hicks, *Letters of Lincoln Steffens*, 1:224.
32. Lincoln Steffens, "Neps," *Transatlantic Review*, 1 (February 1924) :53–55, reprinted in Winter and Shapiro, *World of Lincoln Steffens*, pp. 166–69.

5. AUTOBIOGRAPHER

1. Kaplan, *Lincoln Steffens*, pp. 169, 183; Ella Winter, *And Not to Yield, An Autobiography* (New York: Harcourt, Brace & World, 1963), pp. 65, 69.
2. Winter and Hicks, *Letters of Lincoln Steffens*, 2:585; Winter, *And Not to Yield*, p. 110.
3. Winter and Hicks, *Letters of Lincoln Steffens*, 2:856. Reminded that his father tried to raise him as a free spirit, Pete Steffens said years later, at the age of forty-eight, "Yeah, but I'll tell you something, the world isn't like that. I don't think it works too well, because the world isn't too interested in that kind of person. I was shaking hands and smiling at everybody—I was kind of a California kid, you know. Then I got in the Second World War. I was in the navy for three years." Dusty Sklar, "Radiant Fathers, Alienated Sons," *Nation*, 215 (2 October 1972) :280.

4. Winter, *And Not to Yield,* p. 110.
5. Granville Hicks, "Lincoln Steffens: He Covered the Future, The Prototype of a Fellow-Traveller," *Commentary,* 13 (February 1952) :147–55. See also Daniel Aaron, *Writers on the Left* (New York: Avon Books, 1965), p. 145, and Thomas Cooley, *Educated Lives: The Rise of Modern Autobiography in America* (Columbus, Ohio: Ohio State University Press, 1976), pp. 126–38.
6. Lincoln Steffens, *Lincoln Steffens Speaking* (New York: Harcourt, Brace and Co., 1936).
7. Winter and Hicks, *Letters of Lincoln Steffens,* 2:661, 718, 720, 723, 740.
8. Ibid., 2:755–56, 831; Winter, *And Not to Yield,* p. 127.
9. Winter and Hicks, *Letters of Lincoln Steffens,* 2:916; Winter, *And Not to Yield,* p. 154.
10. Roy Pascal, *Design and Truth in Autobiography* (London: Routledge and Kegan Paul, 1960), Ch. 1.
11. Cooley, *Educated Lives,* pp. 3–8; Richard Slotkin, *Regeneration Through Violence, The Mythology of the American Frontier, 1600–1860* (Middletown, Conn.: Wesleyan University Press, 1973), pp. 94–145, 440–41; Bruce Ingham Granger, *Benjamin Franklin, An American Man of Letters* (Ithaca, N.Y.: Cornell University Press, 1964), pp. 210–13.
12. Steffens, *Autobiography,* p. 77.
13. Ibid., pp. 13–14.
14. Ibid., pp. 14, 153; Winter and Hicks, *Letters of Lincoln Steffens,* 2:733–34, 760.
15. Winter and Hicks, *Letters of Lincoln Steffens,* 2:744, 757.
16. Steffens, *Autobiography,* p. 522.
17. Ibid., pp. 523, 524.
18. Cooley, *Educated Lives,* pp. 9–22.
19. Ibid., pp. 26–49. Cooley's analysis of Steffens's *Autobiography* as an educated life (pp. 126–35) is sparse and assumes, after Granville Hicks, that it only traces the road to communism.
20. Winter and Hicks, *Letters of Lincoln Steffens,* 2:721.
21. Steffens, *Autobiography,* p. 489.
22. Ibid., pp. 15, 34–41.

23. Steffens told his sister Laura that the opening chapters dealt with "unconscious learning." See Winter and Hicks, *Letters of Lincoln Steffens*, 2:745.

24. Steffens, *Autobiography*, p. 109.

25. Ibid., p. 256.

26. Ibid., p. 357.

27. Ibid., p. 414.

28. Ibid., p. 575.

29. Ibid., p. 631.

30. Ibid., pp. 796–98, 809, 815–19.

31. Ibid., pp. 677–78, 693–94.

32. Ibid., p. 873.

33. Ibid., pp 285–91.

34. Ibid., p. 190.

35. Ibid., pp. 386, 446.

36. Ibid., pp. 224–26, 460–61.

37. Ibid., pp. 59–67, 71–72, 150–51.

38. Winter and Hicks, *Letters of Lincoln Steffens*, 2:731.

39. Steffens, *Autobiography*, p. 70.

40. Ibid., pp. 144–45.

41. "Alla Strada Ferrata," *New York Commercial Advertiser*, 11 February 1899, Steffens Papers, Scrapbook 1.

42. Ibid., pp. 672, 760–1; Paul C. Smith, *Personal File* (New York: Appleton-Century-Crofts, 1964), p. 149.

43. Steffens, *Autobiography*, pp. 234–36, 192–96. Cf. Steffens, *Struggle For Self-Government*, pp. 253–60; and Lincoln Steffens, "Two Bosses: Platt and Croker," *Ainslee's*, 7 (May 1901):291–99.

44. Steffens, *Autobiography*, pp. 615–16; Leslie G. Ainley, *Boston Mahatma* (Boston: Bruce Humphries, 1949), pp. 182–84.

45. Winter and Hicks, *Letters of Lincoln Steffens*, 2:724, 727, 733.

46. Ibid., 2:795; Steffens, *Autobiography*, pp. 257–65.

47. Steffens, *Autobiography*, pp. 136–38, 146–48, 292–310.

48. Winter and Hicks, *Letters of Lincoln Steffens*, 1:110–13.

Bibliography

1. WORKS BY LINCOLN STEFFENS

Books

The Shame of the Cities. New York: McClure, Phillips, 1904; reprint ed., New York: Hill and Wang, 1957.

The Struggle for Self-Government. New York: McClure, Phillips, 1906; reprint ed., Johnson Reprint Corporation, 1968.

Upbuilders. New York: Doubleday, Page, 1909; reprint ed., Seattle: University of Washington Press, 1978.

Moses in Red. Philadelphia: Dorrance, 1926.

The Autobiography of Lincoln Steffens. New York: Harcourt, Brace, 1931.

Lincoln Steffens Speaking. New York: Harcourt, Brace, 1936.

The Letters of Lincoln Steffens. 2 vols. Edited by Ella Winter and Granville Hicks. New York: Harcourt, Brace, 1938.

The World of Lincoln Steffens, edited by Ella Winter and Herbert Shapiro. New York: Hill and Wang, 1962. (Contains the full text of *Moses in Red*.)

Selected Articles and Stories

"Sweet Punch: A Monologue." *Harper's* 88 (December 1893):126–29.

"Schloma, Daughter of Schmuhl." *Chap-Book* 5 (June 15, 1896):128–132.

"Mulberry Bend's Tanagra." *New York Post*, November 21, 1896.

"Bloke Murray's Golden Moon." *New York Commercial Advertiser*, December 19, 1897.

"Two Bosses: Platt and Croker." *Ainslee's* 7 (May 1901):
    291–99.

"Hearst, The Man of Mystery." *American* 63 (November
    1906):3–22.

"Eugene V. Debs." *Everybody's* 19 (October 1908):455–69.

"The Least of These." *Everybody's* 20 (January 1909):57–62.

"The Sunny Side of Mexico." *Metropolitan* 42 (May 1915):
    27–29, 55–56.

"Into Mexico and—Out!" *Everybody's* 34 (May 1916):
    533–47.

"Thirty-Threed, A Tale of Our Border Today." *Everybody's*
    35 (July 1916):41–51.

"Making Friends With Mexico." *Collier's* 58 (25 November
    1916):5–6.

"Bunk, A Story of Revolutionary Mexico." *Everybody's* 36
    (February 1917):200–11.

"The Great Lost Moment." *Everybody's* 36 (March 1917):
    350–61.

"What Free Russia Asks of the Allies." *Everybody's* 37
    (August 1917):129–41.

"Rasputin—The Real Story." *Everybody's* 37 (September
    1917):276–85.

"The Killing of Rasputin." *Everybody's* 37 (October 1917):
    385–94.

"The Rumor in Russia." *Nation* 107 (21 December 1917):
    766–67.

"Midnight in Russia." *McClure's* 50 (May 1918):22–24, 60.

"Report of the Bullitt Commission on Russia." *Nation* 109
    (4 October 1919):479–82.

"Neps." *Transatlantic Review* 1 (February 1924):53–55.

"Becoming a Father at Sixty is a Liberal Education."
    American 106 (August 1928):48–49.

"The Influence of My Father on My Son." *Atlantic* 159 (May
    1937):525–30.

2. WORKS ABOUT LINCOLN STEFFENS

Cheslaw, Irving G. "An Intellectual Biography of Lincoln
    Steffens." Ph.D. dissertation, Columbia University, 1952.

Cochran, Bud T. "Lincoln Steffens and the Art of Autobiog-
    raphy." *College Composition* 16 (May 1965):102–105.

Dudden, Arthur P. "Lincoln Steffens's Philadelphia." *Pennsylvania History* 31 (October 1964) :449–58.

Hays, Samuel P. "The Shame of the Cities Revisited: The Case of Pittsburgh." In Shapiro, Herbert, ed. *The Muckrakers and American Society*. Boston: D. C. Heath, Pittsburgh, 1968.

Hicks, Granville. "Lincoln Steffens: He Covered the Future, The Prototype of a Fellow Traveler." *Commentary* 8 (February 1952) :147–55.

Horton, Russell M. *Lincoln Steffens*. New York: Twayne Publishers, Inc., 1974.

Kaplan, Justin. *Lincoln Steffens, A Biography*. New York: Simon and Schuster, 1974.

Lasch, Christopher. "The Education of Lincoln Steffens." *The New Radicalism in America, The Intellectual as a Social Type*. New York: Alfred A. Knopf, 1965.

Rollins, Alfred B. "The Heart of Lincoln Steffens." *South Atlantic Quarterly* 59 (Spring 1960) :239–50.

Shapiro, Herbert. "Lincoln Steffens: The Evolution of An American Radical." Ph.D. dissertation, University of Rochester, 1964.

Stein, Harry. "Lincoln Steffens: Interviewer." *Journalism Quarterly* 46 (Winter 1969) :727–36.

Whitfield, Stephen J. "Muckraking Lincoln Steffens," *Virginia Quarterly Review* 54 (Winter 1978) :87–103.

Winter, Ella. *And Not to Yield, An Autobiography*. New York: Harcourt, Brace, 1963.

3. GENERAL WORKS

Aaron, Daniel. *Writers on the Left*. New York: Harcourt, Brace and World, 1961.

Baker, Ray Stannard. *American Chronicle, The Autobiography of Ray Stannard Baker*. New York: Scribner's Sons, 1945.

Chalmers, David Mark. *The Social and Political Ideas of the Muckrakers*. New York: Citadel Press, 1964.

Cooley, Thomas. *Educated Lives: The Rise of Modern Autobiography in America*. Columbus, Ohio: Ohio State University Press, 1976.

Cox, James M. "Autobiography in America." *Virginia Quarterly Review* 47 (Spring 1971):252–77.

Darnton, Robert. "Writing News and Telling Stories." *Daedalus* 104 (Spring 1975):175–94.

Diggins, John P. *Mussolini and Fascism: The View from America.* Princeton: Princeton University Press, 1972.

Filler, Louis. *The Muckrakers.* New and Enlarged Edition of *Crusaders for American Liberalism.* University Park, Pa.: Pennsylvania State University Press, 1976.

Gay, Peter. *Style in History.* New York: Basic Books, 1974.

Hofstadter, Richard. *The Age of Reform, From Bryan to F.D.R.* New York: Alfred A. Knopf, 1955.

Hughes, Helen McGill. *News and the Human Interest Story.* Chicago: University of Chicago Press, 1940.

Juergens, George. *Joseph Pulitzer and the New York World.* Princeton: Princeton University Press, 1966.

Lee, Alfred M. *The Daily Newspaper in America, The Evolution of a Social Instrument.* New York: Macmillan, 1937.

Lyon, Peter. *Success Story: The Life and Times of S. S. McClure.* New York: Scribner's Sons, 1963.

Mazlish, Bruce. "Autobiography and Psychoanalysis." *Encounter* 35 (October 1970):28–37.

Mazlish, Bruce. "Clio on the Couch: Prologomena to Psycho-History." *Encounter* 31 (September 1968):46–54.

Miller, Zane L. *Boss Cox's Cincinnati, Urban Politics in the Progressive Era.* New York: Oxford University Press, 1968.

Mott, Frank Luther. *American Journalism, A History: 1630–1960.* 3rd ed. New York: Macmillan, 1962.

Nevins, Allan. The Evening Post, *A Century of Journalism.* New York: Boni and Liveright, 1922.

Olney, James. *Metaphors of Self, The Meaning of Autobiography.* Princeton: Princeton University Press, 1972.

Pascal, Roy. *Design and Truth in Autobiography.* London: Routledge and Kegan Paul, 1960.

Regier, C. C. *The Era of the Muckrakers.* Chapel Hill: University of North Carolina Press, 1932.

Riis, Jacob. *How the Other Half Lives.* New York: Scribner's Sons, 1890.

Sayre, Robert. *The Examined Self*. Princeton: Princeton University Press, 1964.

Snyder, Louis L. and Morris, Richard B., eds. *A Treasury of Great Reporting*. 2nd ed., revised and enlarged. New York: Simon and Schuster, 1962.

Spengemann, William C. and Lundquist, L. R. "Autobiography and the American." *American Quarterly* 17 (Fall, 1965):501–19.

Stinson, Robert. "S. S. McClure and His Magazine: A Study in the Editing of *McClure's Magazine*, 1893–1913." Ph.D. dissertation, Indiana University, 1971.

Tarbell, Ida M. *All in the Day's Work, An Autobiography*. New York: Macmillan, 1939.

Thompson, John M. *Russia, Bolshevism, and the Versailles Peace*. Princeton: Princeton University Press, 1966.

Weinberg, Arthur and Weinberg, Lila, eds. *The Muckrakers*. New York: Simon and Schuster, 1961.

Wilson, Harold S. *McClure's Magazine and the Muckrakers*. Princeton: Princeton University Press, 1970.

Ziff, Larzer. *The American 1890's, The Life and Times of a Lost Generation*. New York: Viking, 1966.

Index

Index

Date Due